MR HAPPY

MR HAPPY

**IN THE 60s HE SMUGGLED DOPE
FROM MOROCCO**

**IN THE 70s HE BROUGHT COKE FROM
PERU AND DOPE FROM AMSTERDAM**

**IN THE 80s HE GOT BANGED
UP FOR 16 YEARS**

YOU'LL LIKE HIM

BOB JAMES

JOHN BLAKE

Published by John Blake Publishing Ltd, 3 Bramber Court,
2 Bramber Road, London W14 9PB, England

First published in hardback in 2001

ISBN 1 903402 60 3

British Library Cataloguing-in-Publication Data: A
catalogue record for this book is available from the British
Library.

Typeset by Mac Style Ltd, Scarborough, N. Yorkshire

Printed in Great Britain by Creative Print and Design
(Wales), Ebbw Vale, Gwent

1 3 5 7 9 10 8 6 4 2

Papers used by John Blake Publishing Ltd are natural,
recyclable products made from wood grown in sustainable
forests. The manufacturing processes conform to the
environmental regulations of the country of origin.

CONTENTS

PART ② – THE SEVENTIES

PART ③ – THE EIGHTIES

I can't deny my life has been exciting, and now it would appear that the whole mood is changing towards drugs. It's only a matter of time before certain substances are legalised.

After a lifetime of scamming, I paid society's bill and spend years banged up. I regret the pain this caused to those I love. As for anyone thinking of scamming as a way to get on in this life, I will say this: think a minimum of twenty times first, as things are never, ever as good as they seem.

This book is what happened to me. I'll leave it up to you, the reader, to decide on the rights and wrongs of my life …

Bob James
London, September 2001

PART ①

THE SIXTIES

CHAPTER ONE

MY FIRST SCAM

WHAT THE HELL was I doing there? It was August 1967. I was an eighteen-year-old ex-grammar school boy sitting by the pool at Robinsons beach, one of the quietly cool places of the world, at the Pillars of Hercules just outside Tangier. And, what's more, in the company of the likes of Barbara, the Woolworth's heiress, whom Grant had somehow managed to chat up. We were relaxing in the glorious late summer of the Mediterranean, smoking joints, eating tajine and drinking deliciously aromatic mint tea before heading for Ketama, in the Rif mountains of north-eastern Morocco, to score our first consignment of hash.

Up to the previous month, I hadn't even been out of England – well, apart from two summer holidays in the then small resorts of Calpe and Lloret del Mar in Spain, with my parents, and a school cruise from Venice to Istanbul. Since July David, Roly, Grant and I had been on the road in Roly's Volvo estate. We had driven across France to St Tropez, where we had hung out for a few days with a girlfriend from London whose father owned the trendiest club in town; he was obviously a gangster of some kind and had advised me that I should leave town. Admittedly, we did get rather drunk on rosé in his club. In retrospect, I can see his point – he'd clearly sussed that I was on a scam – but I was heartbroken for at least two days. Still, we were boys on a mission: we were going to do a bit of business. So by the time we hit Barcelona, she was forgotten.

After our stop in Gaudí's wonderful city, we spent two days negotiating the murderous Mediterranean coast road of Spain to the then cool and trendy Marbella. It was beautiful. It only had one street and everyone was on the beach. If I'd known of Dufy's paintings at the time, then I would probably have said, 'It's so very Dufy.' But I didn't, so I simply enjoyed the whole experience as only the innocent coming on paradise for the first time can. We knew a friend of a friend who had a bar on the beach. We had smoked dope and I had eaten fresh grilled red mullet (and nearly choked on the bones) under the stars for the first time. It really was an adventure to sit under a palm roof at rickety tables, hearing the ripple of the Med only a few yards away. I haven't ever been back, but from what I can gather the place I knew is gone. Then again, I suppose right now it is being a magical first experience abroad for someone else, who will be getting equally nostalgic over it in thirty years' time.

We spent a wonderful week on the beach and in the clubs of Marbella. From there we headed down to Algerciras and the ferry across to Tangier, which looked as though it hadn't changed for centuries, the huge, sweeping bay and in the western corner the town itself rising up in steps. It was so exciting and exotic. Africa! Our trip across Europe was great, but this was adventure! Dangerous, but so exciting – the smell of it came to meet us and drew us in.

After a week we felt as though we had died and gone to heaven. I was laid out in surfer shorts on a wheelie sunbed that I thought only existed in French movies. Grant, a twenty-year-old Australian who was the spitting image of Jimmy Page out of Led Zeppelin, was being his usual Mr

Cool, wearing a white PJ Proby shirt, leather jeans and cowboy boots. He was one of those irritating bastards who could wear such things without looking like a prat. I was jealous as hell, but at least you got to pull with Grant around.

David sat under a parasol, discussing the attributes of a Berber rug with yet another carpet dealer he had brought out from town. He was a 6-foot-4-inch broken-nosed public schoolboy with an attitude and an arrogance that I have never seen surpassed. He spent his whole time under the parasol doing deals, stalking the souk (market-place) looking for rugs or trying to find yet another brothel.

Roly was a Restoration character on acid. Instead of just drinking everything in sight he was a walking pharmacopoeia testing kit, and would ingest, smoke or stick up his bum any narcotic. He had been deriving serious enjoyment from the latter ever since hitting France, as every drug you got in a pharmacy from there to Tangier came in suppository form. Now he sat waiting for the next meal, shouting at waiters for yet more drink – dope was only an accompaniment to booze for him. The rest of the time he spent guffawing, bellowing and growing ever redder, roaring at everything that caught his humour with 'Oh! I say!' Which, as everything seemed so alien to all of us back then, happened about every five minutes.

Early that evening, we left the pool, piled into the car and headed down into the souk to meet Mustapha, our connection to Ketama. We had gone to meet him at his spice shop in the souk on our first day in Tangier. Mustapha was the cousin of a carpet dealer whom David knew in London.

He was well educated and came from the Europeanised elite, who regretted the passing of French colonialism. Although his family had maintained their position under the dictatorial rule of King Hussein, it was obvious that he would prefer to be living in Paris than Morocco. Of course, he thought that all European women were sex machines, an attitude common to so many Arab guys, but having said that, he was nowhere near as bad as some.

The meeting with Mustapha was quite straight-forward. We all went upstairs and sat around on the rug-strewn floor of the meeting room, the pungent aroma of the myriad of spices wafting up from below. At our first meeting we had spent three hours negotiating until we had reached a final choice of two prices for our 60 kilos of hash – £10 per kilo in Tangier or £7 per kilo if we were prepared to go to Ketama and collect it ourselves. As we only had £600 of our original £1,000 left, we opted for the latter option. Mustapha had thought we were crazy to go for this, because of the possibility of us being stopped at the numerous gendarme roadblocks between Tangier and Ketama. However, after a lot of negotiating, he agreed to get us cleared with a cousin who was a captain in the gendarmerie as part of our negotiated price. Of course, this was all part of the pretence – at that time the Moroccans were looking for customers and he wanted us to get through. This was in marked contrast to the business practise that was eventually to become *de rigeur* in all dope-dealing countries, especially if you were only buying a few kilos. To wit: they sold you the dope and then phoned the cops, who then busted you, took their share of the money you had originally paid and returned the dope to be sold to the next passing target.

That day was our last day of innocence. In the evening we had dinner in the Hotel Louisanne, where we were staying, and to this day I can taste the wonderful soup de poisson with croutons and roulade we had as we sat and looked out at the lights winking in the windows of the houses that ringed the sweep of the bay below. These were things I hadn't even known existed before I'd left London. We discussed our trip the next day up to the Rif and it was agreed that we would all go up to Tetouan, then David and I would go on up to Ketama to meet yet another member of this constantly expanding family. I never found out if they were all really related, and in truth it didn't matter – they were just good people. We thought the whole thing would be easy from the matter-of-fact way Mustapha had talked us through what we had to do. I remember we had forgotten to ask how long it would to drive to Ketama and in retrospect I can see that our perception of distance – and so much more – was still that of Little Englanders who were used to being able to reach anywhere within their own country within a day. We did not even discuss the possibility of not doing it; we had come this far, and it had been such fun. Besides, those were the days before knowledge and paranoia crept in.

The next morning we were woken once more by the evocative call of the muzzein and had our orange pressé, coffee and croissant looking down over the sweep of

Tangier bay. The ageless joy of the beginning of something totally new. How many adventurers had arrived in this city with the hope of success, from the Phoenicians to the Almahads dynasty heading northward into Spain, on through the Corsairs of the Ottomans and, in more recent times, soldiers of the Second World War?

The drive up to Tetouan was beautiful. It still is. You gradually climb up the edge of the Rif and meander round long bends upwards and upwards. Finally, you round the hills and there is Tetouan. Think of Mykonos and multiple it by ten. It sits in its timeless setting, an organic, living part of the mountains.

We arrived in time for lunch and it was decided that Roly and Grant would stay at this hotel while David and I would drive on into the Rif. We had a peaceful lunch on the terrace of the hotel, which was suspended over a small gorge with a clear mountain stream below swirling and flashing like diamonds as it stormed down to the Mediterranean.

While we enjoyed our lunch, a silence slowly grew between us all as we realised that we were finally really there. I veered from visions of spending the money to fears of a Moroccan jail and considerations of pulling out. Looking back, I think if I had been doing it solo I would have done so at that point and scuttled back to London and a safe life, even though I would have lost my money. However, we were a group of young guys and none of us wanted to be the first to call chicken. I glanced at each of the others and was sure that everyone was having similar thoughts. We drank our red wine in the sun and silence until our musings were broken by a bottle crashing to the floor as a waiter tripped over one of the scrawny cats that slinked between the tables. It had the effect of sparking us back into gear and within minutes David and I were in the car and off. Looking back, I could see the odd couple of Grant the rock star and Roly the toby jug standing under an olive tree with the timeless, brilliant white walls of the town as a backdrop. It was a glorious and funny sight and I laughed as we slid around the corner, onwards and upwards to our destiny at Ketama.

The drive to Ketama was tortuous – the climbing bends that had been such fun earlier in the day seemed to go on forever. We drove through mud-built villages, and every one of them had one house that obviously doubled as a shop: they always had a sheep covered in flies hanging from a post outside, a sight that must have been familiar back in England during the Middle Ages. The further you got from Tangier the further you travelled back in time and by being in the capsule of the car I felt more and more alienated from my surroundings. You certainly were a novelty for everyone you passed – they waved and stared, while the occasional child threw a stone, laughing, as if trying to fell a partridge in flight.

We finally made it to Ketama without passing even one roadblock. We wondered if the dope growers and cops had an unwritten agreement not to go about their business in this hottest part of the day, but it seemed to be a good sign and I was definitely looking for any good omens at that time. As we drove towards the centre of the town, we passed a huge fortified police compound and we glanced nervously at one another, with no need to say a word. I willed myself to be invisible to any insomniac cop. We were certainly beginning to feel the adrenaline flow now, a new feeling then but one that I would come to know time and again over the coming years and, I think, become addicted to.

Mustapha had given us very simple instructions: be in the café between six and seven and we would be approached by his cousin Khalid, who would give us half a dollar bill, the other half of which Mustapha had already given us. These things always sound simple in theory but, as always, the reality of the situation is never so straightforward. We were late, the café was full and I felt as if I had 'smuggler' tattooed across my forehead. The café was full of men in jellabahs – loose hooded cloaks – with faces worn into metaphors of their hard lives on the land. We walked to the bar and, to our surprise, were greeted by a blowsy Frenchwoman of indeterminate age. Initially the situation seemed bizarre, but a quick glance behind the bar resolved the puzzle. There was a framed photo of this woman with a sergeant of the Foreign Legion, who was obviously her husband. They had apparently stayed on after independence, too immersed in this society to contemplate returning to a France they had left so long ago. We ordered beers and sat at the bar, talking to this friendly woman who asked no questions and had obviously seen many like us before. She enabled us to relax and although we were still being glanced at, we seemed to have been given grace, at least for the moment. After fifteen minutes or so, the tasselled curtain from the street was pushed aside and in strode a solid Moroccan wearing jeans and a T-shirt. I knew immediately that this was Khalid and, of course, he knew who we were, but it took him several minutes to walk the few feet from the door to the bar, as he shared a few words with people at the four or five tables between. I presumed he was checking everyone in the bar, for he would know if there was an informer or cop present at once. He finally came to the bar and spoke to Madame in perfect French for a minute or two. As she turned and prepared his mint tea, he put out his hand and introduced himself. As I shook hands I felt a piece of paper in his hand and took it with the necessary subtlety – pretty good considering that his move had taken me completely by surprise.

I went out of the bar to the rudimentary toilet, a hole in the earth floor of a shed. I matched the two halves of the dollar bill by the light coming through a hole in the door and returned to the bar, where David and Khalid were having a very friendly conversation in fragmented French and English. I rejoined them and nodded to David that this was our man. I found Khalid an entertaining and very friendly chap; he had a very open face and his eyes smiled, but I couldn't help but wonder how I could be so daft as to be in this dangerous town trusting my life and liberty to a man I had never met before. Still, it was too late to go back and I did feel OK about this man. We chatted for ten minutes or so and he told us of his several trips to London to visit his cousin, the carpet dealer. He was obviously giving us this information so we would be able to check his authenticity against our knowledge of his cousin and his life. After ten minutes or so he said, 'Shall we go?' We nodded in agreement and left the bar with friendly glances of farewell from the locals. It was obvious that as we were with Khalid we were OK.

Once outside, Khalid, whilst checking up and down the road, told us, 'You will come to my farm and stay the night. We will pack the car tomorrow morning and we will travel to Tetouan together in the afternoon.' This was great news, as we had wondered how we were to be protected from being stopped and how we would make our protected status known if we were. Of course, I was presuming that some of the gendarmes must be straight, but as I would find out, all the graft was put into the pot and shared according to rank. Very democratic.

Khalid guided David as he drove and twenty minutes out of town told him to take the next track on the left. The sky was clouded; all you could see was what was being illuminated by our headlights, and once we were off the main highway, Khalid told David to turn them off. We saw very little and spent our time looking for rocks and bends as we crept along for several miles. Khalid then lent over and pressed the horn three times. Suddenly, 200–300 yards ahead, two huge doors were thrown open and the light from a courtyard flooded out towards us. The light was enough to show that this was one of the fortified farms of North Africa.

These beautiful medieval buildings appear to be nothing from the outside. They are just four solid, plain walls with a few slits and very occasionally a window high up in the wall. As with the fortified castles of Europe, the purpose of such a design was to keep the bad guys out. However, these buildings differ from the European model in that inside they have a warmth and elegance that far exceeds a similar medieval European structure.

We drove through the 15-foot-high oak doors with their beautiful beaten brass hinges and filigree into a large outer courtyard, another pair of oak doors on the far side. We were helped out of the car by an old man who salaamed and greeted us in French. Khalid told us to leave our bags. I presumed that the old man was the gatekeeper. He then returned and swung the outer doors closed – they were so perfectly hung that they required only the merest touch to move them. He then released a rope and a huge bar clanged into place across the doors. The only way you could get through them after that would have been to use a tank.

Khalid went to the inner doors and incongruously rang an entryphone. It made me smile, as it was the same as the one on the door of Roly's flat. The inner doors were then opened and I had never seen anything so beautiful in its simplicity. There in front us was an open rectangular courtyard with small orange and lemon trees and a central fountain. On each side were horseshoe arches leading to rooms. The whole of the place was tiled in a traditional Islamic design of green, blue and yellow. Khalid lead us across this beautiful courtyard and as we crossed I looked up to see astonishingly bright stars. Arabian nights it really was. The place could have been there for a thousand years; its simplicity was perfection.

We then entered the house itself. Rugs and brass tables and you might think of some restaurants, but it was stunning and quite timeless. We were taken into a beautiful room where we were offered chairs, and then Khalid ordered a servant dressed in pure white robes and turban to bring tea. We sat and soaked up this beautiful house for a while, drinking tea and chatting as if we were having cocktails. I felt so at home there at that point and would quite happily have stayed forever.

After a traditional Moroccan dinner of pigeon pastille, Khalid asked if we wished to see the dope and after we had nodded he called for someone. A minute later, a guy came in carrying 10-kilo slabs of Moroccan dope wrapped in Cellophane and two small Moroccan hash pipes. Khalid told us that this sample was from last year's crop, the same pressing as we would be packing in the Volvo tomorrow and that it was number-one quality. He added that we were welcome to open any of the slabs and test them. As we had just eaten a beautiful meal it seemed as good an idea as an Armagnac or Grappa, if not better. So, we unwrapped a slab and heated and crumbled off two pipefuls of the sweet-smelling hash. It was good, with a subtle buzz. The best Moroccan hash back then was really good, a light sandy colour and just a bit stronger than the kif that the Moroccans smoked themselves. Now all you see are Moroccan soaps, which really leave a lot to be desired, but of course quantity is the name of the game these days, not quality.

Khalid did not smoke himself. It wasn't that he wanted us stoned, it was just that he preferred malt whisky. We had a lovely evening and then were shown to our rooms. I fell to sleep relaxed after a tense but eventually fabulous day and smiling at the thought that this adventure business was definitely for me.

The next morning we were woken before sunrise, as we had to get everything packed before midday and get on our way to Tetouan. Khalid appeared in overalls with two of his guys. The five of us then went to work. We removed the seals around all the doors and packed as much as we could in there. As each pack was put in, it was liberally dusted with pepper, as this was believed to be a deterrent to police sniffer dogs. We eventually squeezed in 40 kilos, then removed the bumpers and packed the remainder within these. This was far too tricky an operation for David and I, so we left it to Khalid and co.

Everything was packed and tidied up by 11 o'clock. Khalid's men made sure all of the seals, door panels and bumpers looked untouched by rubbing dust into all the screws so as to hide the fact they had been disturbed and we were on the road by noon, Khalid and I in front and David in the back. We headed back through Ketama, past the lurking police compound, and headed for Tetouan. The wind was coming up from the Mediterranean, blowing dust and sand everywhere. It crowded us into our own minds and because of this we became sensitive to every bend and turn as David and I tensed for the possibility of a roadblock. Khalid was completely composed. For him, this was the same as any farmer in England taking his crop to market. The way the hash had been packed didn't affect the balance of the car, although I was sure that the first police we saw would go straight to it. However, with the need to concentrate completely on the road, such thoughts soon vanished from my head.

An hour into our descent, we came around a bend and there slap-bang in front of us was a roadblock, two 7-ton trucks parked as a chicane. There were about twenty cops with sub-machine guns standing around and sitting in the back of the trucks, looking suitably threatening. Khalid told me to pull over and stop. I was shaking and it required a real effort of will to actually stop it showing. I glanced at David in the rear-view mirror and could see he was on edge, though he was hiding it well behind a slight grin. Two cops in full combat suits moved towards us from the truck. They certainly didn't look too friendly and a few of their companions in the back of the troop carrier nearest us turned and pointed their guns – not raised, but definitely in our direction. As the two cops neared us they split to either side of the vehicle and, without coming too close, shouted out in Arabic and indicated for us to get out of the car. I found the effort of getting my body to act difficult, but I must have done alright as the next thing I knew I was standing facing a young Moroccan who was saying something to me in Arabic. Before I could say anything I heard Khalid saying something over my shoulder. I hadn't noticed him getting out of the car, as I had been so caught up in making my body work. Out of the corner of my eye I noticed that another of the cops was moving round behind the car and now stood covering us from behind. Khalid repeated what he had said and an older cop standing at the back of the truck responded, waving Khalid over to him. He walked the ten yards to the older cop and stood talking to him; then, suddenly, they both disappeared around the back of the truck. I suddenly felt very alone and a very long way from home. It was a situation I had imagined in my mind before, but being here now was gut-wrenching. I leant back against the car and nodded to the young cop who stood watching me. I didn't dare to look at David, as I could sense his tenseness and felt that eye contact would have us both shaking.

From the far side of the truck I could hear Khalid in loud conversation. The volume was rising and I was becoming edgier by the second, if that was possible. I found myself concentrating on the trigger finger of the young cop and hoping it wasn't going to move from its position on the side of the gun.

Khalid's conversation abruptly stopped and everything suddenly seemed still and silent. I'm sure that the world hadn't stopped then, but it had for me. A lifetime later – all of ten seconds in truth – Khalid appeared from around the truck, smiling. That smile removed every bit of tension from me. I knew we were safe and on our way. The older cop who had disappeared with Khalid now appeared and barked an order to the cops covering David and I. These young guys, as they sloped back to the truck, suddenly appeared to me as they really were: conscripts my own age, not the harbingers of doom and ten years in jail they had seemed seconds before. Khalid gestured us back into the car and I leapt in, desperate to get away before anyone changed their mind.

We pulled around the trucks and I saw an officer sitting with his black boots hanging over the side of a jeep. He smiled and shared a wave with Khalid as I accelerated away. I kept looking back in the mirror to make sure they didn't leap in a truck and come after us. As we rounded a bend and they disappeared I finally relaxed, smiled, punched the air and screamed, 'Yeeeeeesssss!'

David and I burst into a chorus of The Beach Boys' 'Good Vibrations' with David bashing the beat out on my shoulders. Khalid looked at us as if we were mad. To him, of course, it had never been an issue that we were in trouble, but to us two callow youths, our lives had passed before our eyes and we were dead and buried.

After our spontaneous outburst we got the story of what had happened. Khalid explained that the captain was not a relative and he was pissed off that their cousin had not paid him and his men their cut for the month. Khalid had agreed to speak to his cousin and that was it. The aggression I had heard was down to my untutored Western ear and probably a few pounds of paranoia.

The rest of the journey was without incident and as we were entering the outskirts of Tetouan, Khalid asked us to drop him off at a crossroads. We were nervous to see our guardian angel go, but we knew we had to lose him at some point and I don't think there would have been much chance of him staying even if we had asked him to. We all climbed out of the car and, with much hugging, thanked him and watched him until he disappeared around a corner. We headed on to the hotel and as we pulled in I looked up to the terrace where we had sat thirty hours and a lifetime ago, to see Grant and Roly waving and smiling. It seemed so odd looking at them. I felt so much older and different to them. I had experienced something frightening and yet so exhilarating that I knew I had started on a road that I couldn't leave now. It seemed to be my destiny and I felt confident that we were going to get this load home safely.

We spent the evening relating our adventures to Grant and Roly whilst getting pissed. Oddly enough, we had no dope. We had been so busy with business that we forgot that Roly and Grant might want to try what we had collected. They were really miffed, as now they wouldn't even know what we were carrying back. At one point, Grant suggested that we hadn't even packed the dope in the car, though we calmed him down over a few more beers. By the end of the evening we had agreed that we would leave for Europe the day after next.

We drove to Tangier the following morning and although we had a clear run we were aware of being surrounded by the 60 kilos of dope. Roly was abnormally reserved and hardly said a word. I could see he was mulling over the same thoughts that I had had two days before. I wondered how he would cope if we encountered anything like the situation that David and I had experienced the previous afternoon with the cops. I was to find out over the years that you could never forecast how someone would react in such circumstances. Only when the chips were down would I ever know, and I would frequently be surprised by the way people could behave at such critical moments.

Roly finally came out of his reverie as we negotiated our way through a herd of goats intent on making it to a stand of thorn scrub. He sat up from his supine position next to me in the back and announced, 'I can't do this. I feel as though I'm going to give you all away.' He went on to explain that he was prepared to forego his share of the profits and that he was going to catch a plane back.

Once he had said it, I felt that that Roly was right. It wasn't that he was being a coward. It was just he did not have the motivation the rest of us had. Although we were young and in it for the excitement as much as the money, there was no doubt that David, Grant and I were more prepared to take the risks because we didn't have the income that Roly had. The three of us half-heartedly tried to convince him otherwise, but we all knew there was no point in forcing the issue; who would want to be passing through customs checks with someone who felt insecure? The worst thing about Roly's decision was that it yet again got my mind racing over the real dangers involved, something I didn't really want. Over the years, I've found that the only way you can cope with these real concerns is to put them aside; if you can't do that, you can't do it. I don't know whether it is stupidity or an ability to ignore the dangers. All I can say is that from that very first trip it was something I could do. I made my calculations and then, once I felt that I was as secure as I needed to be, I would switch into just doing it. I imagine it is like being actor. You become an innocent businessman, tourist, photographer, whatever role you have taken on, to achieve your goal.

Roly's decision also effectively forced David, Grant and I to vocalise our own decisions to continue. After our experience in the Rif the day before, David and I knew that we were now committed and we both knew that we could cope with the pressures involved. Grant, I now realised, was an unknown quantity. It wasn't his fault or anything like that, but David and I had metaphorically been under fire and had come through. Grant had not had such a baptism and I began to worry about him. However, he was full of himself and said he wanted to go ahead. In retrospect, of course, it was crazy that we should have all put ourselves at such a risk. Really only one person was needed to drive the car. However, I think that the fact the three of us bonded at that point enabled us to go ahead; each contributing something the others lacked. I don't think the attributes are definable, but I believe we were subconsciously aware of the fact.

So after this intense conversation we found ourselves in Tangier, loaded up and with our personal decisions made. We had spent the whole trip down from Tetouan sniffing and asking each other if we could smell the dope, so we spent ten minutes trying to find a parking space in the shade once we were in town. It's so obvious afterwards but a small thing like that becomes a major concern when you are actually doing it and takes a lot of time. For instance, we knew that we wouldn't want to be sitting in a long queue on the harbour the next day, boiling in the sun, so we decided that we would arrive early and be at the front of the queue for boarding, even though we thought this would bring us under customs scrutiny for a longer period. Anyway, we decided to be early and, once we had parked the car decided that we would leave it where it was until we departed in the morning.

We checked back into the Louisanne, then wandered up to the Air France office in the main square to book Roly's flight from Casablanca to London the next day. It was a good thing to do, as it gave us all something to occupy ourselves with, and we also had to get Roly organised and off to catch the evening train. It would get him to Casablanca at some unearthly hour but in plenty of time to catch his flight, which would leave before our boarding time and therefore have Roly out of harm's way before we were due to board the ferry to Algerciras.

After Roly had bought his ticket we crossed to the Café Central in the main square; we were a muted bunch, drinking beers, each absorbed in their own world. David was grumbling that he wouldn't have time to buy another rug – this was part of our cover, such as it was. Grant was desperate to get a cab and go see the gorgeous French girl he had had a thing with a couple of nights before. I was wondering what I was going to wear the next day to miraculously turn me into the Invisible Man. Roly was feeling the need to be generous as he felt he was letting the side down. He had said earlier in the day that he would give us the £100 he had secretly stashed and we had quickly accepted his offer as we were going to be very short of money and had worried about the real possibility of not having enough for petrol on the way back. As it was, we knew we were going to have to make a non-stop run to the Channel to save cash. In fact, come to think of it, even if we hadn't been short of money we would probably have done it that way, as by that stage we just wanted to get the business done.

The whole time all of this was going on, Tangier teemed around us. Men in jellabahs held impassioned conver-sations; street kids kept coming to the table and offering us kif and hash; the traffic beeped and skidded. Tangier was so different to the rest of Morocco. It consisted of only a few streets and the medina, which spread like a living entity down from the square to the sea, but it was a fingerhold of Europe in Africa. The last lingering bit of colonial France and the international freeport of the Fifties. All of this was lost to us at the time, though. We had far more important things on our minds.

After an hour in the square we walked back to the hotel and waited for Roly to pack. We all gave him the few personal things we thought we wouldn't want to lose if we got caught, and our address books as we didn't want those being found if we got nicked. We decided not to go with Roly to the station. For some reason we felt we shouldn't been seen together, although it was a bit late now, considering we'd been in the one place in town where everyone was watched all afternoon. So a cab was called and we waved Roly off with cries of, 'See you in a few days!' I was not feeling as confident as I sounded at that time but it was due more to the fact that I was waiting for the journey to start than anything else. I was ready and I wanted to be on my way.

That evening we ate and then wandered down into the medina to see Mustapha as we had agreed before leaving for Ketama. He was great. He asked when we would be coming back and told us how good the new crop would be. We plotted, planned and drank mint tea until ten. As we had to be at the docks by eight o'clock in the morning, we said our farewells and made our way back through those timeless alleys to the new town. Initially, David demurred; he declared himself all in favour of a night in a brothel, although this soon turned out to be empty bravado on his part.

I don't think I slept more than fifteen minutes that night, tossing and turning with doubts and worries but maybe I did, for I was awoken by the early call of the muezzin at about five-thirty, got up and prepared to leave. I spent ages showering and dressing. I had decided to wear a white shirt and jeans with baboush. It sounds crazy, but my logic was that I wanted to look like a tourist but not a hippie. I went to meet David and Grant, who were both ready. David looked like an off-duty soldier: cravat, blazer and twills. Grant was the one I worried about; he looked like a rock and roller. Goodness knows what else I expected, as that was how he always was. I don't think you could have got a more incongruous trio if you had tried. Not a word about any doubts was said between us; we knew we were comfortable in ourselves, and that was what mattered. So we had our breakfast and took our bags and David's six rugs to the car. It just happened that David had the keys, so he was destined to drive us to our first encounter with the powers that be.

It was only a ten-minute drive to the harbour and we were through the dock gates and in a line of five vehicles. The customs shed was quiet. There was half an hour to go before boarding and they didn't seemed to be awake yet, which was great. I was overjoyed to see that the second vehicle in the queue was a battered VW camper driven by a crew of hippies. It was just what we had been praying for, someone else for the customs to pick on. We got out of the car and stood waiting for what seemed an age. Then I saw the customs office door open and three guys in their powder-blue uniforms made their way towards the queue. The car at the front eased forward and we got back into the car as coolly as we could. David said 'inshallah' quietly (the Arabic for 'God willing') and we crawled forward.

What happened next was over in a minute. I saw one of the customs men indicate for the camper to pull over. As it did so, three more customs officers appeared from the office and headed towards the hippies and us. I was so busy watching and shitting myself that they were coming for us, that I only became aware, as we clunked on to the ramp, that David had dealt with the customs. We were on our way and I hadn't even noticed!

We watched the customs men taking the VW to bits as the ferry pulled clear with a blast on its horn. Then we adjourned to the bar. It is only a two-and-a-half-hour journey from Tangier to Algerciras, so there wasn't much time for having a drink, although we definitely needed one. Grant was full of it: 'I must be lucky,' he kept repeating. After our encounter with customs on the road from Tetouan, I rather resented his easy baptism, but what the hell, we were a step nearer our goal, that was all that mattered. We all felt that this next border was the one that mattered, but at least we would be back in Europe when we had to face it. Africa was great for adventure but definitely not where you would want to be busted.

It was such a beautiful day that we went back up on deck. To our left was the beginning of the Atlantic, framed by the Pillars of Hercules. It was an amazing sight; I imagined being there the day that the Atlantic broke in and flooded the Mediterranean basin. Such power and nature in all its pomp. It lead me on to pondering the brevity of our lives in relationship to that of the world. Nothing, a fleeting glimmer of light, and it made me feel good. I only had a mere blink of time for a life and I felt the experiences of the last few weeks were so much more than I had experienced up until now. Not that I had had a bad life, but the raw excitement and that feeling of being at the edge of my senses had already become compelling. All of this philosophical musing made the worries of our encounter to come with Spanish customs seem so small and as we entered the tranquillity of Algerciras harbour I was feeling cool and ready for anything.

David had been in his element for the last hour of the crossing, talking to a Moroccan about carpets. He also seemed totally relaxed and had the air of someone without a care in the world.

Grant definitely didn't have a care in the world. We hadn't noticed, but he had been getting quietly pissed in the bar and I found him sitting in the bar chatting to a bunch of hippies. Well, more like holding court, as was his wont. He was telling them of the time he had hung out with The Yardbirds and they were obviously lapping it up. So we were all, in our own way, feeling and acting very cool as we went to get in the car for disembarking.

'It's a shame we haven't got the VW camper in front again,' I mused.

'You can say that again,' David replied as the doors opened to let in the harsh sunlight.

We rolled off the ferry and into what seemed like an army of Spanish customs. This definitely wasn't going to be as simple as Tangier. The foot passengers and their luggage were already being searched under a tin roof. It was obvious now that the Spanish knew the Moroccans didn't bother too much and therefore they were searching everyone. We saw we were going to be a little while, as the people in the cars in front of us were all being asked to get out while the cars were searched. We sat there very quietly for about five minutes. And then it was our turn.

I felt an old hand at this already and got out of the car feeling relaxed. There were three customs men on us. They seemed friendly until Grant virtually fell out of the back seat. Then they became very brusque and started hectoring him in Spanish. This wasn't much use, as none of us could say more than 'Buenos dias'. I stood quietly watching as two of the customs started manhandling Grant towards an office about twenty yards away. Grant, being a bit pissed and Australian, was not being that compliant but at least he wasn't fighting them. They finally managed to get him through the door and it went very quiet.

The officer who was left with David and I now turned his attention to us. He indicated he wanted our passports, had a glance at our photos and then at us in that accusing way they have, and put them on the roof of the car. He then opened the boot and indicated for us to pull David's rugs out. We did so and opened them up on the ground, whereupon he gestured that we should get the bags out and open them. We obliged and he started rummaging through them. He didn't seem that concerned, but of course he hadn't found anything yet. David then started getting irate, as the customs guy was pulling the odd thing out and dropping it on the ground, giving David a look that said: 'So what can you do about it?' David kept muttering and giving him looks. The officer finished his rummaging, then turned towards the car. Here we go, I thought.

Sure enough, he then went to the spare wheel well, lifted the cover and started opening it up. I looked up to the car in front. The three customs on that one were already feeling down the back of the seats and I started to feel just a tad nervous. Our guy then came out of the boot well and started to move towards the driver's door, but just as he got there his attention was caught by Grant's booming voice as he came lurching through the door from the customs office:

'The fuckers body-searched me!'

He was closely followed by the two customs officers, who were laughing and called something to our man, who himself then started laughing. He moved away from the car towards his mates, who were all in hysterics by now. One of them indicated that we could go. So without being too hasty, David and I shoved the rugs and bags back in, clunked the boot and got in the car. All the time we were doing this, Grant was muttering and giving the customs daggers while simultaneously trying to get dressed. He still didn't have his boots on as I shoved him into the back of the car.

As we pulled away I turned to Grant and asked, 'What the fuck was that about?'

Grant, smiling now, replied: 'They saw a love bite on my bum!'

We all cracked up. The love bite had obviously distracted the customs from any thoughts of drugs and made for a laugh in their boring day. Our luck was still riding hide and we were out of the dock gates now. Another barrier passed.

The next three days passed in a whirl as we hurried across Spain, up and over the Pyrennes via Andorra where, at two o'clock in the morning, we met no customs, and on through Lyon, past Paris. At last we got to Calais and the final barrier – the Channel. We had decided to catch the last ferry at Calais in the hope that the number of customs men on duty would be less and that those on duty would be less inclined to be diligent, as they would be coming to the end of their working day. The adrenaline had been pumping the whole of the day as we neared Calais and it wasn't helped by the fact that we were running late and were starving as we had had only £20 left after Lyon. We had to be sure we would have enough money for petrol and therefore had to go without food for that last rush. Thirty miles from Calais we stopped at a petrol station, emptied a ton of garbage from the car and spruced ourselves up in the toilet. After being cramped up in the car for three days, my body was aching and my mind was numb – which in retrospect was good, as these distractions kept paranoia at bay.

We were so tense by the time we got to Calais that we hardly spoke, and yet despite all our worrying we were waved through without a second glance. It all seemed so easy. All we had to do now was to get through Dover. We sat in the bar on the ferry and treated ourselves to a large brandy each. We were all so tired and hungry that the brandies knocked us out and before we knew it the tannoy was announcing disembarkation. We creaked and stirred ourselves and headed for the car deck.

The ferry wasn't very full as it was the end of the holiday season, and I felt exposed as we clambered into the car. I had drawn the straw to be the driver for this last stage; I was aware of it being Roly's car, and that if anything went wrong they would be looking for him too. The car deck was getting brighter as the cars and lorries switched on their lights and all I wanted to do was to get moving. It seemed an age, but at last we were off.

We headed down the ramp and around to the customs sheds. It certainly didn't look as if British customs were slacking with the last ferry; there seemed to be white caps everywhere. I saw an Alsatian standing with his handler as I swung into the lane they had indicated I should join and I could swear that dog was looking straight at me. If he had barked then I would have broken into a sweat straight away. I moved gently down the lane … and then we were out the other end. No one had bothered to stop us. All I had to do was keep it steady and get out of the gates and we were home. During that two- or three-minute drive to the harbour gates I felt as if I was crossing the Sahara in the midday sun, driving a pink cadillac. Every movement that entered my field of vision was a customs officer coming to stop us. It took forever but finally we were there, out and on our way up the hill, heading for London.

There were no congratulations, we were emotionally drained, all we wanted to do was get home. I spent the next three hours driving through a mist of rain so carefully and diligently that my shoulders went into a spasm as we came into the Old Kent Road. David drove into town and our destination, Earls Court. We expected to find Roly home, but the flat was empty. We were all too exhausted to try and find him, though, and crashed out within minutes of our arrival.

CHAPTER TWO

A BIT OF BACKGROUND 1967

I HAD LEFT college a few months before after a strange two years of studying for an OND and A levels. My family had moved from Southampton to Somerset after I had finished my O levels and I had never really settled into rural life or really made any close friends.

On top of being in an unknown world things were pretty tough at home, as my brother and I were in open revolt against our stepmother, and I left to move into the cottage with Ray and Bradley at the first opportunity. I was supposed to be going to university but it all got lost in enjoying an independent life in a cottage with two other guys.

We had a good few months but we wanted to experience the big world of London so one day the three of us packed our bags and shoved them all into my battered old Fiat and we were off to the bright lights and big city.

Everything went well for about an hour and a half. Then, just outside of Marlborough, the engine blew up in a cartoon cloud of smoke. Luckily we had blown up only about a hundred yards from a transport café and we shoved the car into its car park. Ray decided to go back home but Bradley and I decided to hitch on to London. We sorted out our clothes and packed them into our grotty old suitcases. The one thing that I will always regret leaving behind was my record collection. Fleetwood Mac, Cream, the Spencer Davis Group album – a Christmas gift from Rita the art student, who had taken my virginity and had introduced me to Otis

Redding – all those early Pye blues records and many more that I can't remember. I was to leave my second collection after breaking up with my first wife and still regret abandoning that also. I saw that car sitting there as I hitched to and from London on a regular basis over the next six months. We had told the owner that we would return the next day to collect it. We never could afford to repair it and so I never had the nerve to go and collect my records, as I knew the café owner would want paying for having the wreck sitting in his car park.

Bradley and I decided to hitch separately and meet at the only place we both knew – Paddington station. So at four that afternoon we were sitting in the café at Paddington scanning the Evening Standard 'To Let' section. In those days there were endless pages of bedsits available all over London. We wanted to live in Chelsea and so we found a room in a house Earls Court that was divided into bedsits. Today, by coincidence, a friend of mine has a £1.5-million flat consisting of two of the floors in that very house. The room we lived in is now one of his toilets. It is so strange – Bradley and I lived, cooked on a baby Belling, slept and made love to girls in that future toilet for six months. I often think of a trainee nurse that I had a very passionate affair with, when I'm sitting on the loo now; it makes the time I spend in the smallest room far more entertaining.

We had enough money to pay a week's rent of £10. The only job we could get was washing cars at Shepherds Bush. We were the Russians of our day, working ten hours a day for nothing. It was so cold; my hands never got used it, they felt as if knives were going into them every time I dipped the cloths into the water. You were never dry; water was everywhere, it got inside your clothes and spread like a virus across your whole body. It was alright the first month as it was still warm, but come October the cold was almost unbearable. The customers and the boss treated you as if you were another species – something I had never experienced before. The money was enough to buy a loaf and a tin of beans every night and pay for the bedsit in and a pint of cider in the Six Bells on the Kings Road on a Friday night, where we would go to try and pull. The trouble was, we only had the one room, so we would always have to find out if one of the girls we pulled had a place one of us could go back to.

I finally got a job working in the yacht department of Lloyds register as a clerk. It was still a gentleman's club back then, and maybe still is, and was run by a guy who had been a minesweeper captain in the Second World War, who was always out to lunch. The men who went out and surveyed the yachts were fascinating, but it was not a job I could aspire to as it was highly technical. All I did was file papers, like a humble clerk from a Dickens novel.

I was too busy going out to pubs and watching bands to be interested in that staid old world. After a few months I simply stopped going to work altogether. By then Bradley was working in I Was Lord Kitchener's Valet in Carnaby Street and I got a job working in Gear a few doors down. This was how we began to become involved in the trendy world that we had been hungering for when we left the torpor of Wells. Gear was a shop that sold all the ephemera connected with Swinging London. It was junk really, but the tourists lapped it up. We had such fun – hanging out in Carnaby Street; going to the Speakeasy, where I saw Elton John's first gig in the company of the French girl whose father was later to tell me to leave St Tropez or have health problems; or at The Bag of Nails, where I saw the Four Tops play – one of the greatest gigs I've ever seen. I became very friendly with the brother of the owner of Gear, whom I still see today; the owner himself was cool and looked after us all like family rather than employees. It was through them I started smoking dope on a regular basis. A guy who used to sell jewellery in the street went on to become my longest-standing friend and he was always able to get dope. So, it being the Sixties and Carnaby Street, we were having a ball. I remember we used to walk over to Mr Fish in Saville Row to buy shirts and then up to Stirling Cooper, who made canvas trousers that were stitched in a line parallel with your dick and acted like a codpiece – everybody wore them. It becomes a blur at times and to be honest I can't remember dates and details, but I do remember it was fun! Girls wore the most outrageous clothes and Biba in Kensington, when they opened their emporium in the old Art-Deco store Derry and Toms, was full of girls to pull. We never went home, even after we moved to a small flat near the Hurlingham Club, near Putney Bridge. It was just party, party every night. I ended up running the Gear shop in the

Kings Road, where Marks & Spencers is today, and we spent our time hanging out in the Chelsea Potter, which is still there but a mere shadow of its former glory. It was crazy; people were smoking joints on the pavement, and we spent many happy hours sitting on the benches outside watching the girls. I'll never forget seeing Johnny Binden, a local thug, doing his party piece of flopping his 12-inch dick on the bar and telling the barmaid to 'Take it out of this' when asked to pay for a round of drinks. We would appease our hangovers with poached eggs on toast in the Picasso, which is also still there, before staggering into work.

The Kings Road was fabulous back then, alive with people making and selling the most wonderful clothes. Today we only see the crazy things that are held up as typical of the time, but there was also some amazing elegance. Ossie Clark, who had a shop in Radnor Walk, made stunning dresses for women. A good friend of mine made the most wonderful cowboy boots, a pair of which I still have and wear. Everywhere people were breaking out of the old fuddy duddy world and the Kings Road was at the centre of it all. Everyone seemed to have money and somewhere to live. It really was a golden age. I suppose we were naive, but we weren't to know that it wasn't going to go on forever. And if anyone had told us that it would all end eventually, we wouldn't have believed them. We would probably have simply laughed and rolled another joint.

Whilst working in the Kings Road, I made friends with two guys who were doing a lot of very trendy shopfitting.

I remember they made a wonderful cut-out Silver Surfer for one of the concessions in Gear. Chris and Colin were a wonderful product of the times. They had come to London from Suffolk, where they had been art students eighteen months previously. Chris is still as handsome as he was then; in fact, I am convinced he is Dorian Grey. He had an irresistible way with women. If I'm honest, I was always jealous of Chris as he had that long, straight hair that was perfect for the Sixties look. He was also incredibly thin and fit, which was enough to make you sick without the unavoidable fact that he was also extremely handsome. As a guy I once took to his flat told me afterwards, 'Please don't take me there again. He makes me feel so ugly.'

He was also a very talented craftsman and designer and he and Colin had a successful business doing trendy people's houses and shops. Chris was the business brains behind both this and their dope dealing. The two of them made more money from the dope but the other business gave them cachet and provided introductions into hipper-than-thou circles.

Colin was a complete nutter. Perhaps unsurprisingly, he was a friend of Keith Moon, whom he wanted to be. He had even had an affair with Moon's girlfriend, in an offbeat attempt to become more like the mad drummer. In fact, he had a weird thing with The Who in general, as he had more than a passing resemblance to Roger Daltrey. Colin only ever had two things on his mind: drugs and women. His relationship with Chris was fraught, as Chris was always pulling and Colin would tell anyone who would listen that the girl Chris was with had really wanted him, even if he had never met her. He would even tell the girl concerned this, in front of Chris, which always lead to an entertaining row. Chris carried Colin, as he was a total financial delinquent. If he was ever left holding any drugs, he would immediately proceed to demolish them or give them away at an amazing rate. So he wasn't exactly cut out to be a dope dealer, as even in the Sixties you were expected to make a profit. He also had that other non-attribute for a drug dealer: a habit of always bragging, particularly to women, that he was a drug dealer.

Nevertheless, we really got on and in the end I moved into a flat they had above a butchers on the corner of the Earls Court Road and Brompton Road. I look up at it whenever I drive by today and it still looks as grungy as ever. It was a tip, and made more so by Roly, who also lived there.

Roly was different from us in every way possible. He was the son of a Suffolk landowner and looked – and still looks like – the squire Trelawney in the Sixties film Tom Jones. Today he is a country landowner, but back then he was a lunatic, always up for every adventure. He didn't have much luck with the girls as he was gargantuan, with the dirtiest teeth imaginable and permanently out of it. But none of this mattered, as everyone loved him for his craziness. Roly had an income so he didn't have to work like us three. This was probably a good thing, as he would have ruined any business he was involved in. Mind you, I understand he now runs his own estate, and that of his wife, very successfully.

So there were four of us in the flat, and it was crazy. I don't think a night passed without there being at least ten people in the living room. I remember Syd Barrett sitting there one night in a straight-backed chair; he didn't move or say a word. I think he was tripping, but I'm not sure, as I think I was tripping as well. Chris, Colin and I seemed to have a continual succession of women, although Chris won by a street in terms of their looks and numbers.

I don't know how it came about, but Roly had a friend called Bill who was seeing Jackie, a lovely woman who worked as a hostess in a club in the West End. Jackie lived just around the corner in a mansion block in Brompton Road and somehow or other she and Chris wound up getting it together. Eventually, Chris moved in with her and her young son. So we were all living within yards of one another and it was a hive of activity. Through Jackie we got to know some big dealers and from then on we all started dealing. It was a loose confederation – sometimes we worked together, sometimes on our own.

Roly and Bill knew Grant and David before any of the rest of us, and they had already talked of doing a scam when I met up with them. Chris and Colin were busy with their interiors business and had no desire to do anything like that. For me, a young guy with no serious money, the idea of doing a scam was a dream come true. Drive to Morocco, fill up the car and you were rich. It sounded great to me. David had already done one run himself and he was prepared to introduce us to his people. So we said yes.

I needed £500 for the trip, so I went to the bank and told them I was setting up a record stall … and they just lent it to me. And that's how I came to that first scam with David, Roly and Grant.

CHAPTER THREE

BACK IN TOWN

I WOKE FROM a deep sleep and had to fight my way to consciousness. I lay in my bed, the rain was rhythmically pattering on the window and the sounds of Earls Court going about its business rose to greet me. I looked around my tiny room and everything was different. I lay back, smiled and thought of my new life.

I had left here five weeks before, an eighteen-year-old working in the Kings Road, totally wrapped up in the life of London at that time. My life had been like that of thousands of others back then, but had now been irredeemably changed. I become aware that there was so much more to the world and I wanted to experience it all. I lay there for I don't know how long, seeing the beauty of the Rif and Teroudant, feeling the warmth of the sun, reliving the smells and the people I'd met, the things I had never known existed until now.

Then into my vapid thoughts came the 60 kilos of dope still in the car. I was up and on the phone and within a few minutes had spoken to Roly. I woke the other two and told them, 'I've found Roly. He's in the country at his parents and says we can go up there today and unload – his folks are away for a couple of days.'

Within the hour, David and Grant were off to the country. I was to stay in London, speak to Chris and arrange to give him the dope the next day, as long as he gave us a down payment of half. In those days, everyone who was involved in dope around Chelsea knew one another. Therefore, we had decided on the journey back to give the whole lot to Chris and Colin. They could deal with all the others and they wouldn't know it was coming from us. We were hoping to get £120 per lb. That would work out at £15,840, an amazing profit margin on our initial outlay of £600 plus £100 in expenses.

I was trying to get Chris out of bed from the minute they left, as I only had a few old pennies and I was desperate for something to eat. It seems crazy to me now that I wasn't worried about the business at all right then – I simply wanted a bacon sarnie so badly, and Chris's girlfriend Jackie was always good for a sandwich. After she got up after a night working as a nightclub hostess, that is. I hadn't really got used to the fact that I knew someone who was going out with such an exotic creature. I don't think I actually believed such women existed – I thought they only appeared in movies. Clearly they did exist. The trouble was, they rarely got up before twelve o'clock.

I decided to walk round the corner and get them up. Jackie buzzed me in and came to the door of the flat, looking dishevelled in a green silk dragon dressing gown.

'Where have you been?' she asked me.

I smiled. 'I'll tell you in a minute.'

Jackie was an older woman; she was twenty-six, which seemed a generation older at the time. And, as she was a hostess in a club, she was a woman of the world. I suppose she slept with clients of the £30-a-bottle-of-champagne club, but she certainly never acted the tart. She wasn't a beauty, but she had a certain presence and even though she had a hard face there was a gentle person near the surface. She had set out to get Chris and had ensnared him. At that time it was early days and everything was lovey dovey but over the next ten years it was eventually to turn into a most poisonous and destructive relationship. All of that was a long way off, though. That morning it was good to be with them.

Chris was sitting at the debris-strewn kitchen table rolling a joint, dressed in a dressing gown that matched Jackie's. He looked up as I walked in, smiled a greeting and nodded to a chair. I sat down and then realised I hadn't smoked a joint since Ketama, five days and a lifetime ago. I was stopped from drifting further into reverie by Jackie's voice:

'I suppose you want some breakfast?'

'Please. I'm starving.'

Chris finished rolling the joint and lit up as Jackie pulled bacon from the fridge and put it into the frying pan. Snapper in Marbella had been great but bacon in a pan looked and smelt divine right then.

'So how was the trip?' Chris asked finally.

'Fabulous. We had the most amazing time.'

I spent the next ten minutes reeling off our adventures. I hadn't realised until then how desperate I was to relate them. If I had seen Colin or anyone else first, I am sure I would have weakened and blurted it all out. So it was good that I had come first to the two people I trusted most. When I'd finished, Jackie was smiling and leaning against the sink, puffing on the joint.

'You crafty buggers!' She said, with a laugh.

'You lot were really sneaky. I really had no idea,' Chris added, with a hurt tone in his voice.

I had wondered how Chris would take the news, as we were best friends and we had talked openly of all our doings up until then. I could tell that he was miffed, but he wasn't so annoyed that he would fuck me off. That said, in retrospect I can see that that was the beginning of the end of our youthful intimacy and friendship.

'We agreed not to tell anyone. David didn't even tell Maria,' I replied, somewhat defensively; Maria was David's long-time girlfriend.

'Alright, let's talk business,' Chris said, briskly. 'How much do you want for it and when can I have it? I can move it all, there's been bugger all about for a week.'

This was great news, as we had been dreading coming back to find there was loads about. I felt so good – everything was falling into place so simply. I decided to ask for £130 per lb, seeing as Chris was obviously telling the truth about there being a shortage.

We haggled for a few minutes over the delicious bacon sarnie and a cup of tea and finally agreed a price of £120 per lb. I felt a bit rotten about not telling Chris what I was up to, so I decided that I would knock a bit off when we came to the final settling up. I didn't say anything at the time though, as I thought it would be a nice surprise for him.

That was it. We had cracked it. All we had to do was get the dope to town and we were all rich. The border scares and the paranoia were forgotten; we were home and dry. It sounds so pat now but that was how it happened.

I rang Roly's folk's house and the fat one answered, full of the joys of Spring, telling me the others were in the garage unpacking as were speaking. He said they would call me when they were finished and on their way. I told him to get them to head for Jackie's and that I'd be there waiting for them. Chris and Jackie had to do some shopping, so I made myself at home, smoking a joint and dozing for the next couple of hours.

Three hours later, David rang and said they were on their way and by seven o'clock in the evening the three of them were knocking on the door. They came in laughing with Roly in front, staggering under the weight of two suitcases. It was great to see him and we had a great hug and roar. David and Grant came in red eyed and stoned; they had been rolling joints all the way down.

Roly put the two suitcases onto the green leather Chesterfield in Jackie's front room and flung them open. The sweet, sticky smell of dope that they had brought in with them increased fifty-fold and we all grabbed at the plaques and threw them from one to another, laughing.

Chris became Mr Business. 'Stop fucking about you lot and let's get this lot weighed up so I can pay you and stash it.'

Jackie had a set of greengrocer's scales in her kitchen, which were used for weighing dope. So we carried it all through and the six of us stood around the kitchen table and weighed it off. Of course, there wasn't the right amount. The sixty plaques should have weighed 132 lb, but we were short about a kilo and so it weighed in at 130 lb. Mind you, David had taken a lump off of one plaque, so it wasn't that bad. It still worked out to £15,600 and we weren't complaining.

Chris then went out of the room and returned a couple of minutes later with a paper carrier bag. It was full of small brown paper bags and he handed it over, saying, 'There's seven grand in there. I hope that will do until tomorrow. I'll have the rest by then. I'm going to take the dope and stash it while you count it, if you don't mind.'

The others looked at me for the lead. 'That's fine,' I told him.

Chris repacked the two suitcases and with Jackie in tow left saying he'd be back in half an hour. We had agreed to go to the Hungry Horse in the Fulham Road for dinner to celebrate.

We cleared the kitchen table, sat down with the bag in the middle of table and started counting. It was all in old £5 and £10 notes, so it took about twenty minutes for the four of us to count it all; as we were smoking joints, we had to recount a few of the bags. The money felt and smelt good. I had handled large sums of money before but it had never been mine, so it had always been just a commodity, like potatoes. But this was mine, and it was great. We all kept a note of what we had counted and when we had finished and agreed the total we all sat back smiling.

We sat at the table with the money split into fourteen brown paper bags, each containing £500. It looked like we were sorting out the shopping rather than drugs proceeds. I sat looking at it, wondering what I was going to do with it all. I hadn't even considered that until now, as the whole thing had never seemed real before. Up until this moment it had been a series of adventures and maybes. Now it was real and I didn't have foggiest idea what to do with it.

Before I could come to any conclusions, David spoke up: 'We have to sort Roly's money before we do anything else.' Turning to Roly he continued, 'Roly, we agreed on the drive back that if we made it you should have £2,000. Please don't argue and just take it.'

As he said this, David pushed four of the paper bags across the table to Roly. During the drive back the three of us had agreed Roly deserved a share. We had used his money, his car and without him we almost certainly wouldn't have been sitting there with all this money. We also knew that he would refuse and, sure enough, we spent the next ten minutes talking him into taking it. He acted as if we were being patronising, so we had to keep reassuring him that he deserved a share purely on a business basis, for the use of his car and money. Finally he agreed, adding, 'Alright, but if you need it for the next one, just ask.'

We'd been back a day and here was Roly talking about the next one before we had even finished selling the first load. We hadn't even divided up the money and we were off plotting our next trip. The conversation roared around the world. We were going everywhere that dope grew. Lebanon, Pakistan, India, Nepal, Afghanistan and back to Morocco. I had never thought of these countries except as a lump of dope on a table. No awareness of the culture, religion, climate, nothing except school books. Of course, I knew where they were and bits about them via school imperial history, but I had no actual sense of what they were all about.

The beauty of ignorance. It was adventure; it was wonderful; it was better than sitting in a kitchen in London SW6 on a cold, damp winter's evening. And I wanted it bad.

Our ramblings around the Orient and Asia were brought to an end by the return of Chris and Jackie. Chris came in to the kitchen, looked at us and asked: 'What have you lot been up to? I thought you would've sorted that money out by now.'

'We have, it's fine. It's all there,' I told him.

At this David stood up, swept the paper bags into a carrier bag, including Roly's, shoved the lump of dope in his pocket leaving an ounce or so for Chris and headed for the door. 'I'll just pop back to the flat and put this away and come back for you lot,' he explained.

Roly and Grant jumped up at this and said they would go with him. They were out of the door and gone, leaving me with Chris. He turned to me and said, 'I've stashed it round at Colin's. Before you say anything, it's alright – he's gone off with Moonie until Friday.'

I nodded and started rolling another joint. I suddenly realised that the other three had gone off with all the money. I sat there tired and stoned and a horrible dose of paranoia came over me. I didn't worry about them pissing off with the money. I started worrying that we had been followed all the time and that our pursuers had now stopped the other three and would be coming for us any second. I was really off on one. Thank goodness Chris broke into my thoughts.

'You look fucked.'

I looked up and knew I was. It was all too much, so much had happened, so quickly and I didn't know what to make of it. It was all very well thinking about this sort of thing, but the reality was that it just happened. I hadn't had the time, or maybe the ability, to rationalise it. I put my head in my hands and answered, 'Yeah.'

I wanted to talk but there was so much to talk about – and where to start? I sat there for a few seconds, probably looking very lost. Chris missed all of that and went on: 'I don't know what you're looking so miserable about, you've had it off.'

As he finished, Jackie was in the room all dressed up and doing a twirl. 'I'm ready to party!' she announced.

That was it, any time for reflection was gone. I had over £4,000 to my name and was now a scammer.

* * *

'Well, how do you feel?' asked David as he groaned into the kitchen. He had spent the night at our place. His eyes had that lovely pink hangover tinge and the Moroccan tan enhanced the effect. He looked like I felt. 'Dire,' I replied.

We had spent the evening in the Hungry Horse getting absolutely smashed over their divine fish soup and steak and kidney pies. We had then ended up in The Speakeasy, where we continued until four o'clock in the morning. I remembered with embarrassment un- successfully trying to chat up a delicious girl in an Ossie Clark dress and vaguely recalled that her boyfriend had threatened me at some point. No matter, I had had a great time.

David found a half-clean cup in the sink, made a cup of tea and joined me at the filthy kitchen table. I had staggered to the shops and bought some supplies half an hour earlier and had intended to clean up. But I'd decided to roll a joint first and that was as far as I'd got.

David sat staring into space as the tea brought his brain into some sort of order. I passed him the joint and said, 'I'm going to go and pay off my bank loan and do some shopping in the Kings Road. Do you fancy coming?'

Before he could answer the phone rang. It was Grant:

'Can you tell David that I'm off to Geneva to see Christina and buy a Porsche.'

'So you were serious,' I replied, surprised. I was thinking to myself how crazy it was. We had been paid off by Chris the previous day and here was Grant off to buy a Porsche. A few weeks ago things had been so tight and now we had become so blasé; or was it that it had been pretty shitty not having money and now we were simply enjoying ourselves? People always say guys like us were stupid and noveau. However, that kind of comment always comes from people who have always had money – it's so easy for them to say it and I definitely wouldn't have changed those days for anything.

'I've a cab coming to take me to the airport in five minutes and I'll be back next Friday. I'll only take me two days to drive back and Christina's brother has already got my car. I can't wait to get it and just feel it. It's so cool,' Grant gushed.

'I wish I was coming,' I told him. But I didn't really mean it – he was a crazy driver.

That was the last time I spoke to Grant. He bought the Porsche, came back and was killed when he wrote it off in the Hyde Park underpass the following Saturday. Poor bastard. None of us really believed what had happened. What was worse, his parents wanted the body shipped back to Australia, so there was no funeral. He was gone and that was it. However it didn't take long for his death to be forgotten. I don't think it was callousness, it was just that so much was happening at the time and we were so young.

The flat was a constant hive of activity and people passed through all the time. We had a good friend called Custer, a Hells Angel who was always around and had the first regular supply of coke we knew of. We had tried coke first early in '67 when a friend of Gene and Marty who owned Granny Takes A Trip turned up from New York with it and we thought it was wonderful. Unfortunately, Colin pissed the guy off by dumping a few grammes left on a table into a bin, thinking it was sugar. That's how knowledgeable we were in those days.

This hectic lifestyle of just hanging out and getting smashed went on throughout the winter of '67 and '68. We never stopped and, of course, my finances dwindled rapidly as a consequence. I had not set up a regular shipping from Morocco – I spent too much time enjoying myself. David, who was always a better businessman than myself, had been back several times. He'd organised trips for other people and had now set up a carpet shop in Notting Hill. Come March '68, I was down to my last £1,000 and seriously wondering what to do next.

CHAPTER FOUR

RUGS AND DRUGS IN PAKISTAN

DAVID AND I were sitting in the back of his shop smoking a joint one day when I told him I was running out of money and would have to do another trip soon. I was intending to head back to Morocco and actually get things sorted out for large regular consignments. Before I could say any more, he interrupted me: 'How about Pakistan? Do you remember that mate of Grant's – Roger? He's got a contact there. Remember, he brought that beautiful black back?'

Maybe he had something there. 'Yeah,' I replied, 'why not.' And without any thought I was off again. I really find it difficult now to believe the blasé way we just did such things in those days. I cannot work out whether it was stupidity or just naivety. I would like to believe the latter, but I cannot honestly be sure – it was a different time and place. I suppose what probably motivated me to go to Pakistan was that black Pakistan dope sold for a much better price than Moroccan.

As we continued smoking joints that afternoon, a plan evolved for us to go and see this guy and try to set up a business to ship dope in bulk to England and bring back some on our bodies. We hadn't even done any experiments to see what we could tape to our bodies, or even how to actually do it before we left – that's how organised we were. As for the business idea, we had read, or spoken to someone, about shipping dope in ghee (the clarified butter used in Indian restaurants) and simply presumed this guy would be able to get dope packed in ghee drums. We liked the idea of freighting the dope, as it was safer and we could send a lot more. Why we didn't think that carrying dope strapped to our bodies might be dangerous, I can't say.

David had worked as a graphic artist before we had gone to Morocco and had a real interest in rugs, inspired by his father, who had served in the Indian Army and had collected rugs whilst he was in the East. I had realised over the last couple of weeks that buying rugs had really been David's motivation for suggesting the trip to Pakistan. I didn't mind, it didn't matter to me – I just wanted to do more. I never thought of getting caught. I thought if you did that you would never do it in the first place. Was the real reason some Freudian drive for danger or a recklessness inspired by revolt against social norms? I know for certain that we didn't mind breaking the law because the law was – and is – wrong. Of course, I wanted to make the money but I wouldn't have started smuggling if I had believed I was a dealer in death.

David was to become a good rug dealer and he had made a profit on the six rugs he had brought from Morocco. It wasn't something he had learnt, he just had a good eye and an innate ability in the art of haggling. It has always been a joy to watch him work although it has never been an advantage to be a friend if you wanted a rug as he becomes the dealer in the casbah as soon as the subject comes up. He had already got a couple of dealers to see in Karachi and he wanted to go to Peshawar, which sounded so exciting to me.

We managed to track down Grant's friend Roger, who told us that he had met this guy in Quetta who was really nice and spoke English. He said a couple of friends had been to see him on their way to India and scored. The only problem was that he only had a tea-house in Quetta as a contact point. I don't know why, but we decided to go.

A month later we flew into Karachi at 2 o'clock in the morning and as the plane door opened a wall of hot, wet air rushed in and engulfed us. The smell was all that I could have wished for. It was alien, exotic and exciting and I hadn't even got off the plane. This was going to be fun.

As soon as we entered the terminal we entered a world of chaos. No boards made any sense; people were sitting around waiting, looking as if they had been there since the year dot. Seriously scruffy and overly officious soldiers with loaded weapons were everywhere. We were tired, but it was all exhilarating stuff.

Our driver on the journey to the Intercontinental Hotel was desperate to change our sterling into rupees and kept turning around to harass us in incomprehensible English. I am not a nervous passenger, but this guy, although he couldn't go faster than 40 miles per hour, also didn't believe in stopping for anything. We screamed and gesticulated at him every time he turned around. I don't think he had any brakes and he definitely didn't have a clutch, as the car clunked and lurched at every gear change. I spent the whole journey looking out of the open window, open-mouthed at the novel sights. People sleeping on charpoys on the pavements. By the light from a kerosene lamp over a table in a dingy teahouse it was possible to make out heavily lined features thrown into relief. Faces that had the lines of centuries on them. I had never before seen such ancient-looking people. In England such faces would indicate the people were at least a hundred years old. Yet here, I realised, they would be about forty – it was a tough, tough life. As we got nearer to the city, I saw more and more of what I took to be long sacks of flour or grain lying on the pavements; then one of them moved, and I realised that they were people lying in neat rows, sleeping. I was enthralled at the gentle dilapidation everywhere, which seemed to be the result of some eternal erosion. It wasn't pretty, but it was fascinating to behold.

The Intercontinental was a block of concrete dropped in from Mars. It was modern and horrendous. I have never liked such hotels, then or now. They are the places where people who don't want to know about a place stay. It is their refuge from everything around them, an island of so-called culture away from the peasants. The only good thing about them is that you know the majority of the shits will be staying there, and if you find a good local hotel the chances are that they won't have. I was also to find out that such hotels were the places the drug agencies stayed. They were always the first to treat the locals as subhuman. It really is no wonder that they have never been able to get any co-operation in their attempts to eradicate drugs, as not only are they trying to get rid of the only source of income for most of the farmers but they act like latter-day imperialists with no comprehension or respect for local culture and people.

We tumbled into bed knowing we had to be up in four hours to make our connecting flight to Peshawar. Somehow, we had forgotten that there was a time difference of five hours and were consequently completely disorientated. As we had no alarm clock, we had asked for an alarm call but we were too tired to worry about whether or not we would be woken.

I was dragged from sleep by David pummelling me and shouting:

'Come on. We're late for the plane.'

I got dressed in a rush and was sodden with sweat by the time we got to the foyer, due to the humidity. The receptionist didn't know what to make of us, as I doubt any guest had carried their own bags since the place had opened. We grabbed a cab and hurtled, or what constitutes for hurtling in Karachi at 8 a.m. in the rush hour, to the airport. We needn't have worried, as when we got there the flight was delayed for an hour. This gave David an opportunity to talk to all and sundry. He had this amazing ability to get into conversation with anyone who sat down next to him; even if they didn't speak English he would try. While we sat sweating, waiting for the plane, David engaged a gentleman and his companion in conversation. They wore traditional Pathan costume, which consisted of a pancake hat, a pashmani made of beige wool and baggy trousers of the same colour made of cotton. The man was over 6 foot tall, but wiry. He had a cragged face with inset almond eyes and a nose the size of a toucan's beak. It was truly monumental but it didn't look abnormal; it just meant that his nose was his face. However, he had the stature and presence of a very important man. His whole demeanour meant that you wouldn't dare think of calling him 'beaky'.

David called me over after a couple of minutes and introduced me to Muan Khan. The latter gave me a keen inspection as he held out his hand. He gave it in such a way that I didn't know whether to kiss it or shake it. I thought shaking would be safer, and nearly lost my hand in his iron grip. He was becoming a number before I'd even spoken to him; then he smiled such an open and friendly smile that I was immediately put at my ease. It turned out that he owned a carpet shop in Peshawar and he invited us for dinner the next day and suggested we stay at a hotel, which was owned by a member of his clan. We seemed to have landed on our feet. In fact, things went from strength to strength as we went to the plane with him and his companion and swept through the army guards at the boarding gate without any hassle.

We flew across the desolation of northern Pakistan to Peshawar. The landscape below was the colour of our benefactor's robes, desolate and dotted only occasionally by a village or mud house. I dreaded the thought of having to find my way across this barren land. It seemed as if we were moving further and further away from the modern world we had come from and heading back in time to the 19th century. I also noted that we were the only non-Asians on the flight.

David and Muan Khan had spent the flight discussing rugs. We had asked if he could arrange for us to go to Landi Kotal as we wanted to see the Khyber Pass and he had promised to send a car to take us there the next morning. We landed at the ramshackle airport and if there were any customs we didn't see them, which came as something of a surprise. We were out and into another rust bucket cab which drove us to the hotel.

We collapsed in our vaguely air-conditioned room and slept the vague sleep of jetlag. The late evening call of the muezzin roused us; I awoke thinking I was in Morocco and it took a minute or so to realise I was a continent, or was it two, away from there.

The noise from the street was unbelievably loud. It sounded as if the whole of the North-West Frontier had come to our hotel. Beeping horns and the hubbub of voices called us out to explore the city. We spent the evening wandering the Kissa Khawani bazaar, where you could buy weapons by the truckload, displayed next to the most garish nylon fabrics available on the planet. You'd need dark glasses to check the samples or a heavy migraine would ensue. I just couldn't tell whether the rugs and antiques were genuine, but I doubt they were as every stall had the same ones. David occasionally had a chat at a rug stall- cum-shop, but he said that he would wait until we saw Muan Khan before buying any rugs in the rest of the market. We saw Muan Khan's shop but avoided it, as we wanted to rest and we knew we would be feted for the evening if we entered.

The kerosene lamps gave the whole market a beautiful romantic glow as you moved from under the lamps and outward into the dark and then on into the next lamp's glow. The dark Pathan faces, with teeth showing white in the light, smiled and harassed us as we passed.

An ever-changing pack of child beggars swirled around us like the moths caught by the lure of the stall's lamps. The shock of the first mutilated beggar made me feel sick to my stomach. It was an effort not to stare at the twisted back and the stumps where his arms and legs should have been, and yet he propelled himself skilfully on a rudimentary skateboard. It was as if he was a pollarded and twisted ancient tree instead of a child of ten. I made eye contact and weakened; then, as I drew money from my pocket the whole crowd descended on me. Ever since that experience I have sought to avoid the pricking of my Western guilt brought on by eye-to-eye contact. At least if I avoid meeting the eye of someone in particular, the scrabbling tide is ever-changing as I walk. It has never been easy to harden myself to these beggars and I would occasionally weaken in those early days, but on my infrequent visits since I have steeled myself not to weaken until just before I am returning to a hotel or getting in a cab or rickshaw, or until the last day, when I leave for the airport.

We returned to the hotel after an hour or so and ate an awful meal of lukewarm chicken that had the consistency of rubber. It was interesting, but by no stretch of the imagination edible. We didn't mind, it seemed pointless and rude to expect anything else in such a poverty-stricken environment.

The next day I was woken with a fright by what I took to be a Pathan leaning over me and shaking me awake. Within seconds I realised it wasn't a Pathan, but David. He had got up early, gone to the bazaar and bought a Pathan outfit. It was hysterical – the Kings Road wouldn't know what had hit it in a few weeks' time. Forget the Afghan coats, this was the business. The only problem was, David was just so English. He would have needed a great deal of plastic surgery – well, in fact a complete head swap – to look anything like a Pathan. David, I realise now, had obviously read of Sir Richard Burton's predisposition for adopting native garb and thoroughly enjoyed the masquerade. If he thought he would be accepted as a native though, he was sadly mistaken. We had arranged with Muan Khan to be picked up at 9 a.m. for our trip to the Khyber Pass. I sat in the hotel foyer drinking green tea with my new companion David the Pathan, who sat as if he was a tribal chief waiting for his chauffeur. He was the source of much amusement for the locals, who walked by giggling and nudging one another to look at the crazy franjia (foreigner). I was glad when, after twenty minutes, our driver arrived and we went out to our car, a grubby old Mercedes.

After a crazy day out we came back into the lights of the city from the black countryside and headed straight for the bazaar and Muan. We were dropped at one of the entrances to the warren of a bazaar and wandered around until we found Muan's shop. This time we went in. It was a vibrant cave, full of earthy-coloured rugs. We were welcomed by Muan's companion of yesterday, Muhammed Khan. After the formal introductions to the staff, we started to inspect rugs the like of which we had not seen in any of the other shops the previous evening. Their colours were subdued and natural and the designs appeared to be flowing calligraphy. Even an ignorant like myself knew these were something different. David began to rummage and asked for rug after rug to be laid out for inspection. We sat drinking tea and I drifted into a reverie of what we had seen that day as David discussed the virtues of the various rugs.

After a half-hour or so, Muan Khan came into the shop escorted by two young men and shook our hands warmly. He indicated for us to follow himself and Muhammed Khan up a staircase that I hadn't noticed until that moment, as it was disguised by rugs flung carelessly across the banister. The two men who had arrived with Muan Khan stayed in the shop. As we came to the top of the stairs we found ourselves in a beautiful, if simple, sitting room containing solid but comfortable Victorian chairs and a sofa and strewn with rugs. We sat and idly chatted until more tea had been brought. Once the servant had left, Muan Khan sat back in his chair and, looking at David with a slight smile on his face, said:

'So young gentlemen I can see you have settled in to my city – you appear to have gone native, Mr David. My driver says you were noticed everywhere today.' He gave David a rather pointed look and then continued. 'So, what do you think of my shop? As you have seen, I have excellent rugs, and if there are any other antiquities you wish to see, please ask.'

When the deal was finally done Muan Khan turned to me and said: 'Now Mr Bob, what can we do for you?'

Now, I am not one for jumping to conclusions. However, I knew that he was asking if we wanted to buy dope. I had sensed this was coming. The trouble was, I wasn't sure of this man and I had to respond quickly so as not to give offence or appear to be aware of his subtle inference, so I replied noncommittally: 'Excuse me, but I'm still tired from our journey and haven't been able to properly look at everything this evening.'

He nodded sagely at my response, turned to Muhammed Khan and said something in Pushtu to him. Muhammed nodded in response and left the room.

I wondered what was going to happen next and tried to catch David's eye, but he was studying the weave on one of his rugs. I started to wonder about this man and how things worked in Peshawar. Here I was, sitting with this obviously respected and influential elder who was offering to sell us dope. Before coming I knew that they had dope, though I thought that the process of dealing would be regarded as a bit shifty, but I could see now that it was just business. In Morocco, although it was accepted, you knew you could get into a lot of trouble, and really it was the same here. It was just that we had somehow fallen in at the right level. I doubted whether Muan Khan's power extended much beyond Peshawar but I was leaning towards taking him up on his loosely worded offer. It would save us going to Quetta, and maybe putting ourselves in Muan's hands would be safe.

Then I thought to myself, "Hang on, I've only been here a couple of days and I'm jumping at the first person who even vaguely offers to sell us dope. Is this wise?" My musing was broken by Muhammed coming back up the stairs and speaking to Muan, who then turned to us and announced, 'Gentlemen, I have had dinner prepared for us in a restaurant nearby. So please be my guests.'

As he was speaking he made his way to the stairs and indicated for us to follow. A walk of about twenty yards and we entered what was a bustling tea house, with pots and hookahs hanging from the ceiling. We only caused a slight stir as we entered – this city had seen millions of travellers down the centuries and we were not the sort of travellers to disturb these men from their business and tales.

The food was delicious compared to our previous evening's meal: spicy lamb kebabs and tikkas accompanied by green tea and followed by fruit, while all around the business of the bazaar was being transacted. David was deep in conversation with Muan, which enabled me to look around. As I looked I saw two Europeans in a dark corner looking in our direction. I felt very uncomfortable at their interest, no matter how fleeting; they were too smartly dressed in button-down shirts and blazers for people eating in a bazaar teahouse, and I wanted to go. I thought about excusing myself by saying that I felt sick, but I did not want to offend our host and I decided there was no point in acting in a suspicious way as it would only arouse these guys' interest further. After a couple of minutes, I was relieved to see the two men leave.

We sat and talked about carpets for a while and then Muan brought up the subject of dope directly: 'Gentlemen, I don't wish to appear rude but I believe you are here not just for carpets. I will do all I can to help you if you will let me. Please say nothing now but please feel free to come and see me tomorrow. I have to go now but please stay as long as you wish as my guests. I have left my nephew Abdul outside, who will escort you.'

David and I glanced at each other but said nothing. We exchanged goodnights with Muan and Muhammed and they left us sitting at the table.

As soon as they had gone I turned to David. 'What do you think?'

'Well he must be offering us dope the way he was talking,' David replied. 'I like him and he was very good about prices for the carpets, but I don't know him and we've only been here five minutes.'

'Yeah. I feel as though he's pushing us. And did you see those two Europeans sitting in the corner? I really don't feel comfortable the more I think about all this.'

David gave me a sideways look and didn't say anything for a few seconds. Then: 'Yeah. I saw those guys. I also saw one of them this morning when I was out buying these clothes. I went to look at the Balahisar Fort and as I was wandering around I saw the smaller one come out and get into a police car.'

'Fuck this. I really think we should get out of here and get on to Quetta,' I whispered.

'Yeah. We really should stick to our original plan. I've paid for those two carpets, though, so I'll have to pick those up or it will look really dodgy and we won't be able to get a ticket until the day after tomorrow. So we'll have to play out our cover, at least for tomorrow.'

'I'm not sure than Muan is tied in with those guys or if they were even here because of us,' I reasoned, 'but I tell you, we really haven't anything to gain by taking a risk on this. We've got the guy in Quetta. It's just so pat the way we seem to have fallen into Muan. I am sure it wasn't a set-up meeting him. But just suppose he told them about us and they told him to check us out? Remember, Muan sent Muhammed out when we were in the shop, to supposedly arrange coming here. I suppose it could be coincidence, but I don't know, mate, I reckon we're better off going.'

All the time we had been talking I was getting edgier, as the implications of what we were discussing began to sink in. The awful thing was, we didn't really know anything about this for sure. We could just be paranoid, but what could we do? It just wasn't worth the risk and I found myself checking those around us out of the corner of my eye just that bit more closely.

David's words pulled me back to the table: 'We really mustn't act any different while we're here. If we act cautious, I reckon they'll keep following us while we're in Pakistan.'

'I reckon you should go out and do the photographer thing tomorrow morning and I'll go to Muan's shop and collect my carpets. Then I'll go and book us for Quetta and we'll meet up about 12 p.m. and do some more photography together and see Muan in the afternoon. We'll both keep an eye open to see if we're being followed.'

'Phew! I was just thinking I was tempted to say something when he sort of offered us in the shop,' I admitted, and sat back, looking at the ceiling, saying a little prayer. 'Well,' I continued, after a pause, 'let's get back to the hotel and get some sleep.'

'No. I've got a treat for us and I don't want to miss it,' David replied. I must have given him a very old-fashioned look, as he went on: 'Calm down – it's great. I got Muan to set us up in a brothel earlier and I'm going now, 'cause if we start acting differently, he,' – here he indicated Abdul – 'might get suspicious.'

I couldn't believe this. Here we were with a possible disaster on our hands and he's talking of going to a brothel. The trouble was, he was right. I sat and thought of possible cops, a fit-up and we were off to a brothel. Great stuff, and I sniggered. Although I was not the Casanova type and had never been to a brothel before, like David I was not going to miss out on the chance. In my mind I saw us entering a movie set from '1,001 Nights'. Bejewelled and dark, golden-robed temptresses of the soul calling and smiling resplendent on divans. It seemed pretty cool to me, if a little scary.

David broke into my teenage dreams of houris. 'Well I can see by the look on your face you're up for it. In more ways than one. So let's go.' With that he was up and on his way to the door, closely followed by myself.

A guy no older than me jumped up from a table just outside the door as we emerged and announced: 'I am Abdul. Please to come with me.'

I was full of bravado now and after a cursory look around for the two Europeans who weren't there, we were off with our new acquaintance. I could see as we walked through the bazaar that David, like me, was checking people out as we walked and talked. I thought to myself that it was a bit pointless, as we wouldn't have the foggiest if we were being followed and the light definitely wasn't that good for checking people out. Still, I kept looking as we walked further into the market with Abdul. After five minutes we stopped outside what appeared to be just another anonymous doorway. Abdul opened it with one hand and indicated for us to enter with the other. I might have looked OK, but given the chance I would have legged it right then. I was terrified now that I was actually there.

We entered an empty reception area laid out like a doctor's waiting room. The only difference was that it was very dark, barely lit by a oil lamp turned so low it appeared to be about to flicker out. It took a moment or two for my eyes to adjust and make out a wizened old lady in a sari sat in an overstuffed armchair beside a door. She stirred as if she'd been dozing and looked surprised when, after nodding to Abdul, she saw two European youths in front of her. She composed herself and gave a toothless smile before rising, bowing to us and turning to Abdul. She said something in Pushtu and they both laughed.

'Would you like a drink and to choose a girl?'

'What do you have to drink?' David asked.

After a quick exchange Abdul replied: 'Tea or whisky.'

'Whisky, then,' David replied.

Abdul interpreted again and the old lady bowed and disappeared through the door.

I got a glimpse of a dimly lit corridor before she closed the door and I realised that this wasn't going to be anything like my dream of the Arabian Nights. Abdul indicated for us to sit on a sofa, which I could now see on one side of the room. After a minute or so the old lady returned with a tray on which sat three glasses and a bottle of Johnnie Walker. She poured two glasses, but as she was about to pour the third, Abdul shook his head indicating he was not interested. He spoke to her again in Pashtu and she left the room.

Sitting sipping my whisky, I realised that I had been smelling a delicious musky scent since we had entered the room. It was in stark contrast to the smells we had come across so far in Pakistan. It was exotic, not like the incense we were used to in every dope-filled room in London, and subtle yet filled the room. It wasn't of a particular woman, but of femininity in general; it was delicious and I relaxed back into the sofa and felt good.

It didn't last. A minute later, the old woman returned, shouting at four young women, none of them older than me. They wore loose saris that exposed their breasts and they stood with their heads bowed and their black, black hair lankly falling across their faces. The old hag shouted at the girls again and they shuffled into a line and pulled their hair back from their faces, but the light was so dim that you could hardly make out their faces in the light. They all had the almond eyes of their countrywomen and I could make out what counted for coquettish smiles on their faces, but there was something seedy and nasty about it all. They didn't look as if they were under any duress to be there, but nevertheless I found myself just wanting to leave the place. I don't think it was youthful nerves; it just wasn't a nice set-up. David obviously wasn't feeling any of this. He was scanning the girls, and then asked Abdul whether there were any more.

Abdul spoke to the old woman and then replied, 'No, Mr David. All the other girls are working, but if you will wait ten minutes, madam will get some more.'

David shook his head and turned to me. 'I fancy the one on the end. She has fab boobs. What about you?'

I really didn't want any of them, it was all so tacky. 'No. I'm not interested.'

It was such a shame. The fantasy and the smell really had got me in the mood, but the reality had got rid of my hard-on quicker than a cold shower.

'Go on, it's different and I doubt you'll ever get the chance again,' David urged.

But I was past it now. 'No, don't worry about me. You go for it and I'll sit here and drink some more of this Scotch.'

David shook his head at me and then told Abdul he wanted the girl on the end and that I didn't want one.

Abdul translated to the woman, whereupon she came over, and stood in front of me and went into a right fandango. Abdul translated that I was insulting her house, but I couldn't have cared less and told him to tell her I wasn't feeling well. It did the trick. She ushered the girls out, stood in the doorway and indicated for David to follow her.

After ten minutes David came back into the room and after a bit of haggling he handed over about five pounds in rupees and we left. As we emerged into the bustle of the market, he confided, 'I enjoyed that.'

He didn't say another word on the subject then or later, so I presume that it wasn't a Karma Sutra experience. I didn't say anything, as I had found the whole business so tacky. I couldn't help but wonder if he might have caught something, though, and smiled to myself at the thought.

We said our farewells to Abdul in the square and told him David would collect his rugs in the morning. As we wandered back we decided that we would catch the train to Quetta the next day, if there was one. We knew it was a thousand-mile journey but we felt that if we were being watched that we should do it that way as it would give more credence to our cover of being a photographer and carpet dealer, rather than flying back to Karachi or Islamabad.

My paranoia was stirred up the following morning when we came down to the foyer of the hotel, as there was Abdul, sitting waiting for us. Goodness knows if he had been there all night making sure we didn't skip. However, we exchanged glances and nipped back up to the landing before he saw us.

'Right, that's it,' I announced. 'I'm convinced now something's going on and we've got to get this sorted. I'll take Abdul as a guide for my photography and you go back up to the room, give us fifteen minutes and then go the train station and sort out the train tickets. See if you can get a night train, so we can nip out tonight.'

I went down to the foyer, faked a look of surprise when Abdul stood up at my approach, and said to him: 'Good morning Abdul. How nice to see you. What are you doing here?'

'My uncle Muan asked that I act as guide for yourself and Mr David guide today. Where is Mr David?' he continued, looking around.

'He's not feeling too well and is staying in bed this morning,' I lied. 'I am very glad you are here though, as I wish to take photographs of the town this morning and was wondering whether you would show me around.'

He acquiesced at this, but I could tell he would have preferred David to have been with us. However, he had offered to be my guide and had no alternative to carry out his duties, so we left the hotel.

It was a beautiful experience to wander through the city. I remember seeing the stunning Muhabat Khan mosque, the first I had ever seen; I hadn't even known of its existence before arriving there. All of these buildings and culture were what I wanted to experience before coming, and it was all living up to my expectations. The only problem was the distinct feeling of being sucked into something we had no control over by the chance encounter with Muan Khan and now my guide – or was he my guard? – Abdul, and his cloying presence. Still he was very handy, as he got rid of the beggars and hustlers who accosted us constantly and this was particularly useful when I was trying to act the photographer.

The only problem was, he was pumping me all the time about what we were doing; I just kept up the mantra that

I was a photographer and David was carpet dealer. We wandered the city for a couple of hours and then returned to the hotel. When we were in the foyer I said to Abdul, 'I'm going to rest for an hour and then David and I will come to collect the rugs from the shop.'

'I shall tell Muan Khan and I am sure he will be there to see you,' Abdul replied, with a smile.

'Oh don't bother Muan, I am sure he's a busy man.'

'Oh no. I know he would like to speak to you both,' he insisted.

I knew I couldn't say any more about not seeing Muan, as it would seem odd. I just nodded acceptance, said goodbye and retired to our room.

'Is that you?' David called out as I entered the room.

'Yep and I'm alone.'

'Good. I've got the tickets and the train leaves at ten o'clock tonight, so we've only got a few hours to kill,' David told me with a smile.

I felt a real sense of relief at the news and told him of my wanderings in the city, going into detail about Abdul's digs for info.

'Well, all we've got to do now is to see Muan and pick up my rugs.' David mused.

'If only it was that simple,' I retorted petulantly.

'Stop being such a nervous ninny,' he replied. 'All we have to do is go in, get the rugs and leave.'

I pondered this. 'I don't know. I reckon after the way Abdul has been hassling all morning we will have to be very careful they don't tumble anything. I was worrying while I was out about whether they had been in the room and been in our bags. After all, this place is owned by a friend of Muan's.'

'So what?' David countered. 'The only thing we have out of the ordinary is tape and talcum powder.'

I was getting really pissed at his insouciance by now and shot back, 'They know what smuggling is about and if they've looked in our bags they are going to know we are at it. We are in a country where if they want to they can just stick you in jail forever with no reasons given, so don't just laugh if off. OK, I know we can mumble it, but don't start fucking pretending we are clear yet. Just fucking concentrate and let's work out a way of getting out of any offers for the evening and get on that bloody train!'

David gave me a dirty look but I had at least got him thinking constructively rather than just assuming everything was going to work out without us doing anything. He lay back on his bed and started working out options. 'Maybe we should pretend to be interested and agree to go and see him again tomorrow,' he mused. 'At least that would get him off of our case long enough to get gone.'

'Yeah. That's not bad,' I agreed. 'I doubt if they would be that bothered if we didn't turn up tomorrow and they don't know our surnames. Or do they? It wouldn't be that hard for them to check the passenger list for that flight if they were that interested. Still, I suppose those European cops wouldn't bother until they got some hard evidence from Muan that we were at it.'

We sat and worked our way through alternatives, but really that was the best we could come up with. So we set off for the bazaar ready for any more offers of help from Muan.

As we walked into Muan's, one of the assistants greeted us with smiles, told us Muan was waiting for us upstairs and led us up. We walked into our worst nightmare. Muan was sitting talking to the two Europeans of the previous evening with Muhammed standing behind the sofa. The four of them turned to us and smiled. Muan Khan indicated for us to sit and said:

'Good evening, gentlemen. I would like to introduce you to my friends, Chris and Jahn from Holland.' The two of them rose and we were introduced. David looked as nervous as I was, but we kept it together, wondering what would come next.

We didn't have long to wait. 'I believe you gentlemen have something in common,' Muan continued, 'and I thought it best if I got you together and introduced you. I am maybe wrong in this, gentlemen but I believe you are here to buy hashish and I have been helping Chris and Jahn here to do the same. However, they have had a little problem with the police that I was able to help them with.'

David started to say something but Muan was in full flow. 'Please, Mr David, you do not have to say anything. Let me finish what I wish to say and then you may say what you wish. My friends here are in the business and would like to discuss things with you.'

We both knew then that they were cops.

David, bless him, turned to the two of them and said, 'I

was going to say to Muan Khan that I'm not feeling well tonight but that I was out for a breath of fresh air and thought I would collect my rugs. So, if you don't mind, could we leave talking until tomorrow? We'll come here about twelve and have some lunch.'

With that he got up and within in a couple of minutes we were on our way back to the hotel. We packed, paid the bill and got a cab to the station. We had a good laugh as we sat on the Quetta train, thinking we would be well on our way before they knew we were gone.

The next day we arrived in Quetta, which was just a small town back then. It is surrounded by hills and has a stark beauty. We found a room in a restaurant with rooms above on the main street. Quetta was, and still is, in the middle of nowhere. Its importance is military, due to its proximity to Iran and Afghanistan. (I didn't know it then, but in a few months I would be 150 miles away in Kandahar, across the border in Afghanistan.) We knew we wouldn't be staying long. It sounds crazy now, but we had no phone number or address for the man we had come to see. We were told to go into a teahouse in the main street and leave a message for him there.

So, after dumping our bags, we walked down the main street and found the teahouse. The proprietor spoke English and told us our man, Abdul Muhammad, would be there the next day. There was nothing to do in the town and we felt very noticeable, as we were the only Europeans as far as we could see. Walking down the dusty street, we felt as though we were in a Western movie.

We ate another of the most horrendous chicken meals I've ever eaten that night and, sure enough, we both were in serious trouble the next morning. Leaving the hotel, we went down to the teahouse terrified that we would have a major bowel accident. David and I must have looked very comical walking down the street with our bum cheeks tightly clenched. All we wanted to do after all our troubles in Peshawar, and now this, was get done and gone. We went into the tea-room and knew straight away that the man sitting in the corner was our man.

He was in full Pathan garb and had a rifle leaning against the wall next to him. 'Mean' doesn't really sum him up; 'lethal' is probably better. There we were, two English hippies suffering with the squits, and we had to talk to a man who looked as if he would shoot you as soon as look at you. The proprietor confirmed our guess and nodded us towards him. I was not that comfortable with the situation at all, and I definitely wanted to be somewhere else. In fact, anywhere else.

We introduced ourselves and our man stood. Both David and I were both over 6 foot and this guy was the same but it was his hands that caught your eye – they were huge. He extended a hand, into which mine, at least, disappeared almost completely. Then he smiled and said, in perfect English, 'Very pleased to meet you.'

Now, this was totally unexpected. Even though Roger had told us the guy spoke English, it just didn't seem to fit his whole demeanour. It turned out that Abdul had studied geology in London ten years before and knew the city well.

We sat talking about Camden, where he had lived for about five years – a rather incongruous subject to be discussing in the middle of Pakistan, I felt. Still, it settled us all down and he invited us to his house near Zharat the next day.

We had to make a dash back to the hotel as soon as we had made the arrangements for the next day. I'm afraid I didn't quite make it. Cool drug dealers? My arse.

The next morning, we were picked up in a battered Merc and driven towards Zharat, a hill-station in the mountains. After an hour we turned off the road and, following a ten-minute drive down a track, came to a modern bungalow set amidst fruit trees. Abdul Muhammad was there to greet us and we all sat at a table on the veranda that ran around the bungalow. A veiled woman brought us tea and fruit. We sat and looked out onto a beautiful, if austere, valley covered in fruit trees; it was idyllic. The one thing that strikes you in such places is the quiet. In England, even in the country, you will occasionally hear a car or a plane passing overhead. Nothing like that distracts you in places such as that corner of Pakistan, and it was wonderful. It made the whole conversation of trying to smuggle large quantities of dope into Britain so easy and made any problems seem so easily solved. We brought up our idea for shipping ghee and that was ruled out. However, Abdul explained that his family shipped a lot of dried fruit to a company they owned in Karachi and that he was sure he would be able to sort something out. He was really keen to secure a deal, as no one he had met up until then had been interested in doing business on a large scale. We felt as if we really might be able to make this one work. So, after a beautiful day sitting in such an idyllic place, we returned to Quetta on top of the world.

Before we left, Abdul Muhammad said he would drop the 20 kilos we had asked for to the hotel the next morning. He said we didn't have to worry about strapping on to return to Karachi, as there were no customs inspections on internal flights.

The next morning Abdul arrived early, as our flight was at twelve. He brought the 20 kilos in a box. Clearly, he had been very busy overnight. He told us that he was able to do everything we had talked about and that we should return to London and set up a company. When we were ready we were to telex through an order for a shipment and that he and his partners would send it. He was also prepared to give us credit on the first 200 kilos, as he was so keen to get started. We were really pleased, stuck our 10 kilos each in our luggage and set off for the airport.

We were walking to the Fokker Friendship, the plane that is used for internal flights, when I noticed all the luggage on the tarmac and three policemen standing by it. I didn't give it much thought, as I presumed that they were just guarding it. However, when we were halfway to the plane the first passenger arrived at the luggage. I figured from the gestures of one of the cops that he was asking this guy which was his luggage. He pointed at a case and then he and the officer were heading back to the terminal. This I didn't like, as our dope was simply wrapped up in our cases, and if we were pulled out we were in poo poo. We couldn't go back, but I was feeling distinctly uncomfortable as we drew nearer. The second cop then asked a guy about five rows in front of us which was his luggage and the two of them were shortly on their way back to the terminal too. That left one cop and about ten passengers as potential search targets – and we were two of those ten. I was feeling distinctly uncomfortable at that point, but I realised I had to act normally at all costs. As I came level with the cop he looked me in the eye and I remember smiling. He nodded me on. David was right behind, so I waited to hear if anything was said. As I put my foot on the first step to the plane, I heard a voice close to my ear:

'Excuse me, sir.'

At the same moment as thinking 'oh fuck' I realised it was David. What a bastard.

We collapsed in our seats and couldn't even have a drink – no alcohol on flights in Muslim countries – which was a real shame, as I was a little in need of a strong drink after our experience.

When we got to Karachi we were able to get ourselves on the following day's flight to London. All we had to do was strap on the dope and we would be home and dry. So the next morning I stood stark naked while David strapped the plaques of dope to my body and in the process turned me into a living mummy; it looked hysterical. One thing we hadn't realised was that your body hair was pulled as you moved. My pubes had been well taped down, so as I moved the pain was excruciating. It wore off as a few of the hairs were pulled out; the only trouble was, it seemed as if they were being dragged out one by one. To start with the dope was very stiff, but after half an hour it had warmed up and had moulded to my body pretty well. I felt very comfortable, apart from the fact that I couldn't do up the top button of my trousers, as I had plaques taped across my back that ended below the waistline. So, I sat naked, covered in dope and Elastoplast, acted the tailor and moved the button. God knows what anyone walking in would have thought. If I couldn't have done it up, I would have had serious problems. These little things sound so trivial, but over the years it has always been the small things that have caused mishaps.

After David had strapped me up it was much quicker doing him. The last thing we did was cake ourselves in baby powder. When the cleaner arrived she would probably think there had been a baby powder fight in the room, as the place was covered in talc. All done, we checked out of the hotel and headed for the airport feeling pretty good.

I would like to say we had no problems. And I can. We simply sailed through Pakistan customs and then we were at Heathrow and walked through without a glance from those customs either. To say we were ecstatic in the cab driving into town would be an understatement; we were laughing and punching one another all the way to David's shop in Notting Hill. That said, the first half-hour there counts as one of the most painful of my life; when we were pulling the tape from our bodies we must have taken 90 per cent of our body hair off. God, it was agony.

Anyway, we'd done it. We sat smoking joints to kill the pain until the evening, then staggered to Julie's across the road for a celebratory drink. Life was good; I was truly Mr Happy.

CHAPTER FIVE

THE AFGHAN DEBACLE

CATHY WAS DAVID'S girlfriend and we all fancied her but I didn't expect to see her naked opening the door that morning. I'd only come to collect some money from David.

'Come in,' she said standing naked in the hallway and in no rush to pick up her robe from the sofa. She was obviously enjoying showing me her small, slim body and pert breasts.

'The envelope on the mantelpiece is for you,' Cathy said, turning to show me her gorgeous body yet again and then drawing the veil of the robe across herself.

'Thanks,' I replied. As nonchalantly as possible, I crossed to the mantelpiece, opened the envelope and glanced inside. 'Is David here?' I went on, hoping the answer would be no.

'No. He's gone to Dorset for a few days. Do you want some coffee?' Cathy asked, smiling and heading for the kitchen.

'Sure. I'll roll a joint.' I sat down trying to adjust my hard on.

Cathy was a hooray and a real raver. She was one of those girls who just wanted to have fun for as long as possible and had remarkable stamina. She worked for an art gallery sometimes. I could never work out if she did real hours, as she seemed to be out and about all the time looking stunning no matter what time she'd been up till the night before. She was Pre-Raphaelite in her looks, with porcelain skin, and she always wore swirling chiffon clothes. Not really my type, but that morning she exuded a sensuality that I found impossible to ignore.

I rolled the joint on a Buffalo Springfield album that I'd found on the coffee table amidst the debris of the night before and surprised myself by saying, 'Do you fancy some lunch?'

'Yes please,' came the reply from the kitchen.

I finished rolling the joint as Cathy returned from the kitchen, put the coffee on the table and sat next to me. I lit the joint and sat back, looked at Cathy and knew that this was my lucky day.

I passed her the joint and she snuggled back on the sofa, at the same time moving so that our thighs were touching; by now I was certainly radiating excitement. We were sat there not saying anything in words, sharing the joint for a few minutes. Then, when the joint was finished, I stubbed it out in the ashtray and, feeling relaxed by the joint, turned and kissed her lightly on the lips. There was no resistance and we both laughed and then kissed again. We never got to go for lunch, but spent the afternoon in bed.

About 6 o'clock the phone rang and Cathy answered it. When she came off the phone she said: 'We'll have to get up, my brother's coming over. But don't go – we can all go out together for dinner. You'll like him.'

Her brother Steven arrived and I was introduced as one of David's friends. Steven was a tall Aryan hooray with soft eyes and a very quiet manner. I found this really unusual, as most of the hoorays I had met were really noisy and arrogant. David had talked of Steven to me before. A few months before, he had arranged to sort Steven out in Tangier if he could get down to Morocco with a car. In fact, David had been pissed off, as he had gone down and waited for three days for Steven, then found out from Cathy that her brother had crashed the car in France, fracturing a few ribs and damaging his ligaments.

We had a joint and went on to Finchs in the Fulham Road for a drink and then to Nikita's in Ifield Road for dinner. Over the meal, Steven started talking of his aborted trip to Morocco and how he really wanted to go now that he had recovered from his accident. He came over as a really nice guy – a little shy, but OK. The three of us got nicely pissed and had a good time, though as the evening wore on I began to hope for a return trip to bed with Cathy. However, I couldn't push things because of the possibility of Steven saying something to David. Steven put me out of my misery – when we got the bill he said that he was going home to their parents' place. I said I would drop Cathy off on my way home and she gave me an approving smile which told me we would be sleeping together.

When we had said goodnight to Steven and climbed into the cab we immediately fell to necking as only young people do, deep, lingering and going on forever. I felt like doing it in the back of the cab – thank goodness we were only ten minutes from her flat in Queensgate. We were there and in bed making love within fifteen.

The next morning we were lying having a joint when Cathy asked, 'Would you take Steven on your next trip?'

I had been thinking of going to Afghanistan for a couple of months after reading A Short Walk in the Hindu Kush. It fired my imagination to meet these people who had never been conquered. Not only that, but the dope was great. I had talked to David about it, but he had plans to go to Lebanon to buy carpets. None of us knew of anyone in Afghanistan to score from, so I was a little dubious of going on my own and had put it to the back of my mind until then. I lay there with Cathy stroking my chest and, without even thinking about the pros and cons, replied, 'Yeah why not.' It was a crazy thing to say, but I had just had a beautiful night of sex with Cathy and felt so good that the words just slipped out.

Cathy rang Steven while I was dressing to leave and told him that I had rung her and asked to meet him. She arranged for me to meet him in the Roebuck on the Kings Road at lunch time. After we had kissed goodbye she told me, 'We won't be doing this again.' And we never did. Nobody ever knew of that day and night of sex. By the time I saw Cathy again it was five years on. She was married to someone I didn't know and had a child. We shared a look and a smile when we met after all that time, but it was in a restaurant and she was with a girlfriend and so was I. That was the last time I ever saw her.

Steven and I met as arranged in the Roebuck and ten minutes later, over a beef sandwich, I asked if he fancied going to Afghanistan. He jumped at the offer. It was crazy, but as I've said before, that's how things seemed to happen back then.

We booked tickets that afternoon to leave on November 20, just ten days later. We spent most of those ten days together poring over maps, making vague plans and smoking joints. I didn't really get to know Steven that well, but it didn't seem to matter as we were only going to be together for two weeks and we had the excitement of a scam in our brains. The only preparation we made for winter in Afghanistan was to buy two sets of thermal underwear each. That's how organised we were.

The day of our departure came so quickly that before I knew it we were in Beirut waiting for the Ariana flight to Kabul. I knew we were heading into the wilds when we sat with the other passengers waiting to board. They were a serious-looking bunch of tribesmen on the whole, wearing the dress the rest of the world knows so well, following the sickening civil war and the refugees whose numbers are still growing here. There was also a spattering of well-dressed Afghans, obviously government officials returning, who kept themselves apart from their countryman.

It was strange travelling with Steven, as on every other trip we had gotten into conversations with people. However, I realised Steven wanted to keep apart from new company. I thought he was just nervous and left it at that, hoping he would relax once we arrived in Kabul and become more convivial as it was all part of what our trip was about. I found out later that the plane was the only one that Afghanistan's national airline had. It showed. As soon as you boarded, you got an idea of where you were going, a certain grubbiness but with warmth. These days airlines are all much of a muchness, but back then you really did get a foretaste of what was coming as soon as you boarded a foreign plane. The flight to Kabul crossed endless deserts and the occasional mountain range. I don't remember seeing one city during the whole flight. It was just a journey to the back of beyond, which only added to the excitement I felt as we finally came in to land at Kabul airport, which looked more like a hangar than an airport. As always when arriving in a new country, it was the smell that confirmed I was somewhere else.

After a two-hour wait in the airport to get our visas, we went to The Park Hotel, just around the corner from the bazaar. On the drive in, the city seemed to me to have a more medieval feel to it than anywhere I had been in Pakistan. It sat in a bowl of hills and was bloody cold – an unpleasant surprise that I would learn to live with over the next few weeks. The surrounding hills were covered in snow and the wind was cutting. Amazingly, there were more camels on the road than cars. I remember the women in black chadors, which looked like prison bars rather than an item of dress. The other thing I remember particularly vividly was the number of Mongol faces we saw. It really brought home the fact that this city was part of the old silk route and that this junction on the road from East to West was still functioning. It was bustling, full of people in transit. I was desperately keen just to wander in this amazing crossroads of the world.

We checked in and were straight out. You could never call Kabul a beautiful place in terms of its architecture, such as it was; its beauty lay in its energy and mystery. In fact, it wasn't really a city, more a collection of villages and throngs of people. As a westerner, I knew that this was a place I would never truly be accepted in, as soon as I started wandering around the stalls. You were just another passing customer to the timeless merchants of the bazaar. Steven and I were certainly targeted straight away, but not by beggars. I think it was the fact that it was not yet a place that saw a lot of tourism, so an industry of begging had not evolved there yet. There were a couple of street urchins who hustled us as we left the hotel but nothing like I had experienced in Pakistan, where it had been ceaseless.

The bazaar was teeming in the early evening and it was wonderful to smell the kebabs and spices. Steven was still very wary at every approach that was made to us. I was becoming very worried about his approach, as he seemed to draw attention to himself by being so nervous. We wandered for a while but he was so twitchy that I had to agree to return to the hotel with him after only half an hour.

We had left the hotel so quickly on our arrival that I hadn't taken it in. It was very basic but clean and there was hot water. However, when we went to get something to eat the place was full of hippies and we found ourselves being approached by a wild-looking guy who dumped himself down at the table and immediately started telling us about how he was stuck there and couldn't pay his bill. I really wasn't interested, as I could tell he was going to try and tap us for money, but Steven seemed to find the presence of another Englishman reassuring and they got talking. The guy had been on the hippie trail from London through Europe, Turkey, Iran and now Afghanistan for six months, and he had fallen out with the people who he was travelling with. They had slipped away one morning a month before, leaving him stuck in Kabul. He was obviously desperately trying to borrow money to leave but I didn't have enough to sort him out and just wanted to get away.

I made my excuses and headed for our room, determined that we should leave Kabul the next day as I could only see trouble coming from this guy. I lay on my bed; after an hour Steven returned. He was so caught up in this guy's problems that I really got pissed off. I realised that Steven was frightened about the real reason why we were there and had got himself involved in this guy's problems as a way to avoid thinking about it. So I had to tell him that I thought we should leave Kabul the next day and head up to Bamiyan to see the Buddhas as this was part of our weak cover of being photographers – our story if we were ever asked what we were doing in Afghanistan by the authorities. I couldn't tell Steven that I knew he was afraid, as I knew he would deny it and it would simply put a rift between us. I definitely didn't need that now we were there.

Steven couldn't say he didn't want to leave, because if he did he knew the guy would be on his own – and he couldn't handle that. So we agreed to get up early and head north to Bamiyan. However, I went to sleep with a distinct feeling of unease that night, realising that I was with someone who wasn't really up for it. I determined to have it out with Steven on our trip to Bamiyan as to whether he wanted to go on or return empty-handed. I figured we could have it sorted out before returning to Kabul and then heading down to Kandahar, where we had agreed to try and score our dope.

We were up and on the road early the next day in a clapped-out old Mercedes with a nutter of a driver who we had hired for three days to take us to Bamiyan for $30 plus fuel. The guy on reception had given the driver instructions in Pushto before we left. That was our only communication with him, as we had no Pushto and he only knew 'Yes' in English. Getting out of Kabul was a series of hooting and shouting but once we were on the main highway it was fine, as the road was empty and the views stupendous.

Those three days going to Bamiyan were a memory that will live with me forever. The valley itself is beautiful, and the Buddhas magical in their majesty. By some weird coincidence, on the day I write this the Taliban have started to destroy the Buddhas of Bamiyan. To think that no one will ever see those stunning statues again makes one want to weep. They sat in the valley towering above the plain, timeless and awe-inspiring, yet so gentle and poetic. I cannot believe that these disgusting bigots of the Taliban could do such a thing. However they are not the Afghans I knew. They were created in camps in Pakistan and are as far from the true Koran as any fundamentalist

Christian is from true Christianity. I find it hard to be surprised at the Taliban's destruction of cultural heritage, though, as they have wiped out so many of their own people in the name of their religious fakery.

Back in '69, I had my own problems – trying to deal with Steven, who was a nightmare every time I tried to talk to him. I was at a loss as to what to do. What I wanted really was for him to say that he was going to return to London on our return to Kabul, but he would never admit to being nervous and became full of bravado at my slightest suggestion that this might be the case. I was only twenty and didn't feel confident enough about my interpretation of the situation to just tell him to go back, so we returned to Kabul with the vague agreement that we would stay over one night, hire a car and head south to Kandahar the following day.

We ended up spending an extra day in Kabul because the hotel had to find a driver who would rent us a car for five days – car hire didn't exist then. Amusingly enough, we gave the guy $100 and that was the end of it – no insurance or driving licences. Such things didn't exist. If you owned a car in Afghanistan, that was enough to make you legal.

We drove to Kandahar the following day across a flat plain with the Hindu Kush like a sleeping, glistening monitor lizard on our right-hand side all the way. I think we probably saw three other vehicles all day. The only incidents occurred when a man or boy would wave from the side of the road, yet there was no human habitation for miles in any direction. We stopped once for a pee and a man on a bike appeared, stopped, gave us the once over, nodded and then crossed the two-lane highway and was away to somewhere that didn't exist. I'm still not sure whether he was real or not.

The only good thing about the drive was that Steven seemed to relax for the first time. It is no surprise really, as although it was a long, flat road, the scenery was timeless and you could feel a sense of the countless armies from Alexander to the present day that had marched across this plain, heading for the wealth of the Indian subcontinent only to be foiled by the Afghans.

We came into Kandahar late in the afternoon. It appeared to be a very plain and squalid town. As we headed for the centre we came to a roundabout, which was rather odd as it served no obvious purpose, and saw a sign for a hotel in English. Following the sign, we pulled into a drive that lead to a grubby grey house set amidst dusty trees. It didn't look too appealing, but we knew we wouldn't find anything better elsewhere, so we went in. It was reminiscent of a filthy youth hostel but there was one redeeming feature: we were greeted by a pair of middle-aged twins smiling through huge moustaches. They spoke in laboured English, which was nonetheless wonderful to hear, and showed us a room that had eight metal-framed beds in it and in the centre a large wood-burning stove. It was freezing and the blankets had obviously not been cleaned this century. Still, we stayed, as we would be the only inhabitants of the room and the twin brothers were just so nice. Within an hour the stove was burning and we had been asked to eat with the brothers.

We ate in what was clearly the family living room. The food was brought in by a heavily veiled woman, whom we were told was their mother. Within minutes we were asked directly if we wanted to buy hashish. And that was it. We had made our connection, and what a wonderful connection it was. The brothers, Badar and Shir Khasaid, said they would take us to see the hashish the next day.

The next morning we were taken to what must have been a grain store at one time. It was a large stone building with nothing in it except a hundred or so sacks stacked in one corner. When I entered the building, I was instantly overpowered by the smell of hash. It was awesome; I felt stoned straight away. It was as if the air was mixed with a treacle of hash; it rolled over us and slaughtered me. Badar took us over to the sacks, opened one and the smell grew even stronger. He took a handful of the pollen from the bag and rubbed it between his hands and it just became a lump of hash; it was so full of resin that it just congealed. He explained that this was from their farm in the mountains to the north and that it was all first-grade hash. I knew that it was better than anything I'd had ever seen other than Nepalese by just looking at it, and started grinning, I had died and gone to hash heaven and that was fine by me. Even Steven was smiling, which made a nice change.

We spent the next few days sitting in a swing seat in the garden of the guesthouse smoking dope. I can't really tell you much about it other than that I was giggling continuously and I had the idea for a cartoon strip based on Badar and Shir Khan and the hotel. We had also decided to come back in the spring with a couple of Land Rovers under the guise of being a photographic expedition, fill them up with dope and drive back. After all, it would only involve driving across half of Asia and Europe – a simple thing to do. Well, it seemed to be when thinking about it stoned.

We made a couple of forays into town and I do remember making it to the Chel Zina, which was supposed to have been carved out of a huge outcrop of rock by Babur, the founder the Moghul empire. I sat there looking south towards Quetta, where I had been only four months before. I wondered how things were with Abdul Muhammad, and laughed. We had set up the company and sent out an order for raisins. But we had never received a reply.

On our last morning Shir came in with a sackful of hand-pressed plaques of their beautiful dope. They made them by putting a sheet of metal over a fire, then taking a handful of pollen, putting it on the sheet and heating it through. Then they removed it and flapped it from one hand to the other, rather as a pasta maker would do, until they were wafer-thin plaques. It was so beautiful the way the plaques sat in your palm so you could feel the shape of the maker's own hand. Hysteria descended when we came to weigh the dope, as we were talking in kilos and the twins were talking in Afghan weights, of which we had no comprehension. The scales themselves were a hoot, being merely a length of wood with a pan at either end. We reckoned that we had 30 kilos when we had finished weighing. To our surprise, after the business had all been settled, the brothers gave us a present of something I had never seen before. It weighed about half a kilo and was like a deep ochre honeycomb. I was bowled over when Shir said it was opium, pronounced 'affium'. We were surprised and a little nervous of taking it, as it was classified as a class-A drug and if we got caught bringing into the UK it could lead to a harsher sentence. But we wanted to try it, so we took it. You do some crazy things in this life, especially when you're stoned. We paid the twins $1,500 for the 30 kilos and swore we would return in the spring with the Land Rovers. We waved as we drove away and I never saw them again.

We got back to Kabul and it was chaos. Pakistan and India had started fighting and Europeans and anyone who wanted out of Pakistan were having to come to Kabul as all the airports in Pakistan were closed to commercial flights. The Park was jammed with people. Thank goodness our room had been reserved for us, or we would have been in a jam to body-pack before our flight the next day.

We spent that evening trying to find out what was happening with the flights, with no joy, so we simply had to turn up at the airport and hope. The following morning we were up early and strapped the dope on our bodies. I still can't believe that I managed to strap 15 kilos to my body and into my cowboy boots, but I did. I must have looked like the Michelin man. We arrived at the airport and it was madness. There were people everywhere. This was a good thing for us, as there were no security checks, although there were a lot of soldiers about.

We checked in and were told the flight was delayed an hour. Now this was serious shit, as our connecting flight from Beirut was due to leave three hours after our arrival and if we missed it we would have to get another flight or stay over in Beirut, which wasn't something I fancied, being strapped up with all that dope. We figured we'd have to go, so we headed for the gate. The next thing I knew, Steven was talking to Sandy Gall the ITN reporter. It was surreal, I couldn't believe it. I heard Steven agreeing to take two sacks of film back for Gall. Then I thought, that's not a bad idea as we could pretend we were working for ITN. So we boarded the plane with a sack of film for ITN in London and new job descriptions: war correspondents!

The flight left at the rearranged time and for half an hour everything was fine. Then the pilot came on and told us we were stopping at Istfahan, in Iran. Now I was getting very worried. I really didn't want to be nicked in Iran, but unfortunately there wasn't nothing we could do about it. We landed and were herded into a transit lounge – a great relief, as it meant that at least we wouldn't be going through customs. The trouble was, I was starting to get really hot and the odour of dope was wafting up out of my shirt. I wasn't too worried as we were prepared for this and had large tins of Johnson's baby powder in our camera cases. So off I went to the toilet, chucked a load down inside my shirt, patted it down and came out of the cubicle. Thank goodness I looked in a mirror before returning to wait for the plane, as my face looked like a Japanese geisha – it was completely powder white. I quickly ducked back into the cubicle and wiped it off.

After an hour we were called back to the plane, but I knew by then that we had missed our connecting flight to London. Steven was in a real state and started going on about how we would have to use the ITN film as a way of getting on the next flight to London when we got to Beirut. I told him to take it easy and that we would just have to see how things went.

We landed in Beirut at about six o'clock and as soon as we touched down we were told there were no flights to London until the next day. The next hour was one of the most horrendous of my life. Steven went onto some other planet. Instead of just leaving the airport and going to a hotel he went berserk telling everyone he could speak to that the film we had was due on TV in London and that we simply had to get on a flight back. It was insane – we had been told there were no flights until the next day, but he just wouldn't accept it. Of course, the reason was that he couldn't handle the thought of having to come back through customs the next day loaded up. The trouble was, I couldn't get him anywhere on his own for even a few seconds. It sounds crazy now, but we were the only people in the airport and he was raving on in front of all the staff he could find. It was a nightmare over which I had no control; I sat on a bench by the front door trying to pretend I wasn't there.

Finally he gave up and we got a cab into Beirut and a hotel. I was furious and I wanted to kill him for his stupid antics. However, there was no point in worrying about it now. We had other problems. For one thing, we would have to remove the dope from our bodies and then put it back on the following morning and we had none of the hospital-size Elastoplast left. We would have to buy some more in town, and both of us couldn't go out of our room in case someone came in and found the dope. So we got to our room and, with a lot of wincing due to the plaster pulling our body hair off as it came away, we stripped the dope from each other.

We ordered dinner in our room and afterwards I went out onto Alhamra street for the first and last time. It was to be completely destroyed in the civil war that started a few years later. Under different circumstances, I would have been enjoying every minute of being there. At that time, Beirut was known as the Switzerland of the Middle East and was a pretty outrageous town, but all I wanted to do that night was find a chemist, buy wide Elastoplast and Johnson's baby powder and get back to the hotel pronto. I found three chemists, bought their whole supply of Elastoplast and baby powder and, making sure I wasn't being followed, went back to the hotel. Of course, the question of why anyone should want to bother following someone who bought Elastoplast and baby powder didn't enter my head. I had been through a rough day and was running on adrenaline. I got back to the hotel and went to bed and fitful sleep.

The next morning we went through the whole palaver of strapping the dope on again and set off for the airport. Steven was once again in a nervous state, which worried me, but again there was nothing I could do except reassure him that everything would be OK. We checked in and waited to be called for our flight. As we were waiting we noticed that they were doing hand baggage checks so we decided to go through separately. I went first, passed through with no problem and went down to the departure lounge.

I was sitting in the departure lounge for about five minutes, during which time there had been no sign of Steven, and I started to worry. I sat there for another five minutes, by which time I knew something was wrong and decided that I had to get rid of the dope. I figured that I would go to the toilet, dump it in a bin and just get on the plane and get home. There was nothing I could do for Steven if I was stuck in Beirut too. As I got up to go to the toilet I heard my name being called to go to security, I rushed into the toilet and began stripping the dope from my body. When I was halfway through stripping it off the door of the cubicle flew open and I turned and found myself looking down the barrel of a handgun. I was busted.

I was taken to the police office and there was Steven looking hangdog. He burbled out that they had patted him down and found the dope. Then he told me something I couldn't believe. He said they had taken him to the luggage for the flight and asked him to point out his friends' luggage … and he had pointed out mine. At this the cops had laughed and said thank you. They told him they had tricked him into giving me up as they had no idea he was with anyone at all. Mr Happy I wasn't.

CHAPTER SIX

BANGED UP IN THE LEBANON

I **OPENED THE** kitchen door to be met by the smell of gas and the sight of Mum with her head in the oven and her body contorted across the floor. During the years since, I have often felt thankful that her head was turned away from me so that I am not haunted by the sight of her face in death.

Then my dad was behind me and pulling me away, shouting, 'Go and get Auntie Vi!'

He shoved me and my brother back toward the front door. Then we were running. As we ran we could hear Dad's fading screams of, 'Jean! Jean!'

I awoke to hear myself screaming, 'Help me, Mum!' I had never prayed before or since to my mum for help, but I did that night in 1969. After coming around, I realised that I had been dreaming of my Mum's suicide six years earlier and remembered where I was. I was huddled on a bench in a squalid holding cage in Beirut police station – they had brought us here from the airport. And now I understood what had brought me out of my dream. It was someone screaming in agony, a nerve-jangling sound that had stopped abruptly. We looked at one another with absolute terror. I saw that Steven's face had drained white and he slumped in tears on the bench. I felt as if I was going to throw up, but before I could two cops appeared dragging a sodden man who was whining and trying to keep all the weight off the soles of his feet, as they were two bleeding masses of pulp. The guards threw the man onto the floor of the cage, swore in Arabic at him, turned and walked away, laughing. The man looked at me with absolute terror in his eyes and started to speak in a frantic whisper between tears of pain. I couldn't understand a word of Arabic but I knelt next to him on the filthy floor and tried to calm him with my pathetic French. However, he wasn't listening, he was in too much pain; I now know that he was praying. I started to try and look at his feet but I had nothing to clean his wounds with and was thinking of tearing up my shirt to use as rags when the two guards returned, and waving their guns, indicated for Steven and I to get up and come out of the cage. I was physically shaking now, thinking they were going to take us for beating.

We were led along a dimly lit corridor of cells and from every one we heard crying and moaning; I felt myself begin to crumble. Then the guards threw open the door to a cell, pushed Steven in and slammed the door. I realised that they were just locking us in cells away from the beaten man. I felt a wave of relief, but it only lasted for a moment or so before I was shoved into a small cell, barely illuminated by a low-watt bulb in the ceiling, with a hole in the corner that stunk of sewage and a stone bench to lie on. I sat on the bench and shivered with cold and fear.

I sat for five minutes just shaking and wondering if they would return to collect to me for a beating. Then I started to think a bit. If it was going to happen, it wouldn't be tonight. We had been held at the airport all day and it was now late evening, maybe nine or ten. I was wearing only my Granny Takes A Trip jacket, jeans, shirt and cowboy boots; it was a cold December night in Beirut and I was freezing. I could still smell the dope on my body and Afghanistan seemed a century ago. My teeth actually rattled in my mouth with the cold and the terror of my unknown fate. I slumped into a ball on the bench and begged God to get me out of this. My only other concern was what effect my arrest would have on my father. I lay there thinking how it would hurt him and knew he would not understand.

I felt so stupid about having agreed to bring Steven with me. He had brought all this on us, I was sure, by spending all that time at the airport hustling the airlines. I should have walked out of the airport and left him, but I stayed and now I was fucked. The night passed with the screams and moans from beaten prisoners terrifying me as to what would happen to us the next day. I could hear prisoners shouting to one another in Arabic; I tried to shout for Steven, but I heard nothing in reply, so I went back to the bench and curled again into a foetal position. But then I had to get up again and walk to try and keep warm. I was so frightened that I didn't feel tired. My mind constantly reeled through the horror of my situation.

I'll never forget the door opening after I don't know how long – twelve, maybe thirteen hours – and a guard with a smile handing me a cup of Turkish coffee and a pack of three biscuits. I knew then I wasn't going to be beaten and felt a wave of relief roll over me. A gesture, a smile, can evoke so much more than words, and I smiled back in gratitude. Of course, on reflection this same guard would probably be beating (and, as I was told in the main jail in El Ramel, electrocuting) other prisoners later in the day. He slammed the door shut before I could say anything. I ate the biscuits and gulped the coffee in seconds and slumped back onto the bench.

An hour later we were in a court being interviewed by a magistrate, as they used the Napoleonic Code in Lebanon. There was nothing we could say really, as we had been caught with the dope on our bodies. After an hour we were loaded into a jeep and taken to El Ramel. Now this was an experience. We were taken in through huge gates to a squalid, fetid prison. It was the pits, it stank and the guards were armed and dangerous. They looked on us as scum and we were really shitting ourselves as we were led, carrying two rancid blankets and wearing our own clothes, towards the cells. We were taken into a corridor with four doors and through the 6-inch hatch in the door of the first cell came shouts in Arabic and hands jammed out, pleading with the guards. I didn't like the look of this. The guard unlocked the next door and we were shoved in. I couldn't believe it: suddenly there were sixty men before me shouting, in a babel of languages, 'Hi, when did you get busted?' We were in a room full of all the non-Arab prisoners. It was crazy, 90 per cent were in for dope. It was more like a convention of dope dealers from all over the world than a prison.

The room we found ourselves in was about the size of a large living room and I couldn't work out how everyone could sleep in there. I was to find out that night: with difficulty. Nevertheless, the relief of being with people we could talk to was wonderful. Within an hour of our arrival we were told what would happen to us. We would end up getting a three-year sentence and be released after about eighteen months, as that was what happened to any foreigners caught with less than 100 kilos of dope. And indeed, that was what happened eventually. We settled in and were fed by the other guys. Everyone had a story to tell. Tom the American was caught loading 200 kilos onto a yacht at Jounieh. Steve the Australian dropped about an ounce of Red Lebanese in front of a cop and was promptly arrested – he ended up doing a year. Three English guys known as the Chillum brothers had been caught in full Arabic gear in a camper at the Syrian border; the tank loaded with 70 kilos fell from their camper as they went to pull away after being told they could go.

Everyone was fine, except for one sad American who had obviously completely cracked up. He sat in the corner sobbing and moaning; it was tragic. The problem was, he had been like that for several days and the guys couldn't get the guards to do anything, so everyone was very on edge. It had been agreed before our arrival that when the guards came to do the evening count, everyone would sit on the floor instead of standing to be counted.

There was one Lebanese guy in with us, Samir, who was put in to act as interpreter. He was to become a good friend. He had the job of telling the officer in charge of the count why we were all sitting on the floor. This officer was known as Mickey Mouse and Tom would sometimes throw his voice during the daily count and squeak

'Mickey'. The officer used to go berserk, and we loved it. Sounds stupid I suppose, but we were desperate for entertainment in there.

When the officer and the six guards with M16s came to do the count it appeared to me that all hell broke loose between Samir and the officer. However, I was later to learn that it was a normal conversation by Lebanese standards. Eventually, Mickey Mouse and the guards stormed out. Samir turned and said Mickey had agreed to move the sad guy out. The following morning he was gone; nobody knew what had happened to him. That was to be a big problem during my stay there. You met people, then they were shipped with no warning and you never knew where they had gone; only occasionally would a message come via a returning Lebanese of what small local prison the diaspora had been moved to.

That evening I found out how I was to sleep for the next eighteen months. Once the count was done, thin mattresses that had spent the day rolled up to be used as chairs were rolled out to cover every inch of the floor and with personal possessions used as pillows everyone settled down to sleep. It was something you never really got used to; someone would snore in your ear or you would get a toe up your nose, or someone would scream in their dreams. But we coped. It was to get better when I was moved from the central jail, as the cells weren't so crowded there.

In retrospect, it was amazing that we kept our spirits up in such circumstances; we didn't whinge and anyone who did was given short shrift. We played poker and backgammon or plotted scams all day. Every day we sat in the sun for an hour and after that isolated experience at the police station we never saw any further malicious treatment of people. Sure, there was indifference from the guards, but we got by and we had many laughs amidst the squalor and filth. Talking of which, one of the first things you had to learn was how to wash your bum over the hole in the floor when you had finished going to the toilet, as there was no toilet paper. (Another thing about those hole in the floor toilets: you were always aware of the rats down there.) We even managed to get hold of some wire and botch up a heated coil run from the light socket in the washroom to make coffee. Crazy – I can't understand how no one was electrocuted.

I only remember one real pain, and that was Marty, an American who thought he was it. There was a concrete set of shelves at one end of our mass cell and he climbed up and lived up there for a couple of days like one of the stylites, extreme religious recluses who abounded throughout this area in earlier times. I don't think he was basing himself on them, but he did smoke banana skins, which he claimed to get high from. The guards dragged him away to the lunatic asylum after a few weeks, more for the fact he got on everyone's nerves than for being crazy. We all thought of getting shipped to this mythical fabulous hospital until Jann, a Danish guy who had been sent there after acting crazy, came back and told how the majnoun (crazy people) just wandered around there with no supervision. He told us he had seen two stabbings in the week he was there and when he was told he would be getting electric shock treatment he made a miraculous recovery and got himself shipped back. So that option was out.

The one thing you dreaded was getting sick. There was no treatment of any kind and luckily no one got really sick while I was there. I went to the dentist once for a toothache and before I knew what was happening he'd pulled the tooth out without anaesthetic. Christ that hurt, but luckily I never had another toothache during my stay.

We were allowed to buy food from the shops that must have been outside of the gate. Something that will sound odd was that we were allowed to keep any money on us that we had when we came in. If we didn't have any cash we could eat from the two buckets of fassoullieh (chickpeas and a couple of bits of lamb stew) and pitta bread that were brought in every day.

We were kept totally isolated from the Arab population, as they definitely thought all of us hippies would have a subversive effect on them. I think they were right too, as we really didn't give a shit. Although the conditions were diabolical, there was no feeling of being an inferior being. You had been caught and you had to do your time and that was it. No petty nastiness, as you'd find in a British prison.

We were continually at war with Mickey Mouse, though. I remember one night I was lying unable to sleep, as I had someone's foot in my face, and I looked up to the windows. Suddenly, through the four barred windows, I saw the muzzles of M16s appear. As I was about to shout, the door flew open and a platoon of armed guards tried to come in, shouting and screaming. Of course the only trouble was that as we were all over the floor up to the door, they couldn't get in. While they were shoving people out of the way to get in we were all swallowing our dope and flinging any contraband we had away.

Finally, some order was restored and we were all shoved out into the exercise yard semi-naked. We knew there would be trouble as we had started to try and dig through the wall in one corner. It wasn't the most brilliant of escape plans, as we would have had nowhere to go even if we could get out and over the wall. Still, we went ahead out of boredom more than anything else. After twenty minutes, Samir was called and we were all made to stand up in the yard with spotlights on us. Mickey Mouse then started shouting and when he had finished, Samir translated that we would be staying in the yard for two days as punishment. It wasn't much fun, as they only gave us buckets for toilets and we had no clothes or bedding. The only good thing about it all was that we were totally stoned as we had swallowed our stashes of dope. I think I probably slept for half of the time we were out there, so it didn't really matter, and it was summer so it was a lot cooler than being in the sweat box of a cell.

Finally, in the summer of 1969, Steven and I were taken to court and given our three-year sentences. I remember around this time we heard that the Americans had landed on the moon. It was so strange to look out of the barred windows high up in the wall and see the moon and know that there were men standing there. I felt that we were not even as near to the real world as they were.

Within a week Steven had been shipped out and I hoped I would be sent to the same prison as him. We doubted it though, so we said our farewells and hoped to see one another in a year or so in England. I stayed for a couple more weeks and then one day they came and told me to pack up. I said goodbye to the guys I had become close to, including Samir, and I was gone.

I was loaded into the back of a Land Rover with two guards and we trundled off. I'll never forget seeing the Mediterranean that sunny day; it was beautiful as we drove south on the highway the Israelis would trundle up years later to wipe out the Palestinians of the Sabra and Chatilla camps. We turned off the highway after awhile and headed inland and up a mountain. We drove right to the top, to a small village and a tiny prison. The prison only had twenty men in two cells. I was shoved into one of the cells and was very nervous about my reception. The guys in there couldn't believe it. They looked at me as if I had come from the moon, amazed at seeing a European in their cell. One of them came and spoke to me in French, which I could hardly understand, and then showed me a space where I was to sleep right next to the open sewer which was the toilet – and it stank. Still, I had no choice. Using a combination of French and gestures, he told me that when someone left I would move up the line and eventually would end up at the top of the room. I didn't fancy the set-up too much and I was hoping to get moved to where Steven was. If I could find out where they had taken him.

It was late evening and the inmates were all unrolling their bedrolls and settling down for the night. I noticed that they all had mosquito nets strung from any convenient peg or window bar. I thought that meant there was going to be some fun, and there was. I was kept awake all night by the damn mosquitoes and by the following lunchtime I was blind due to the swelling of a host of bites that covered my face. The screw who brought the bucket of fassoullieh was spoken to by the prisoner who had initially spoken to me. He came over to me and, after looking at my face, left. Five minutes later he was back with the sergeant in charge of the prison, who took one look and said he was moving me. Within an hour I was hurtling down the mountain I had only come up the day before. I thought I was going to die as, being blind, I had no warning when we came to the hundreds of hairpin bends and was thrown all over the place; I had a vivid memory of just how close to the edge of sheer precipices we had been the previous day. Within half an hour I could tell we were in a small town, as we moved slowly and then stopped. A guard helped me out of the jeep and I was led into another prison. I could see nothing and was finding it really difficult to walk without stumbling while carrying my bedroll and the carrier bags full of my stuff. Then I heard Steven say, 'What the hell happened to you?' I was so glad to hear him. I told him what had happened and he led me into what was to be our home for the next year.

After two days the bites had subsided enough for me to be able to see again. I was told that the one person I really had to become acquainted with was a man called Abou Monsur. He was a Palestinian who had served in the British army at the end of the war and still spoke in a military-style English, and was the boss of our cell. It was so much cleaner here than where I had been. The prison consisted of six vaulted cells all identical, about 20 feet long with an iron gate at one end, which was connected to what looked like aisle in a church. It wasn't a church though, it was a very old building from about the 15th century that had been turned into a prison. At one end of the aisle was the guards' room, kitchen and a visiting room and a large metal gate that lead to the real world. At the other end there was a door that led to a yard about 30 foot square, which we were allowed to sit in for two hours a day. The only thing we could see from the yard was the sky.

When I saw Abou Monsur, he did not disappoint. He had a large military moustache and stood erect with military bearing. You could tell he was a bit of a conman, but he was also a very nice guy and had really helped Steven settle in. It was a good job that he had, as there was one guy called Kalim, a Palestinian, who was a member of Black September and very definitely bad news. He regarded us as devils incarnate and had had a go at Steven on his arrival. He spent the next six months ignoring us and we never made any contact with him, which was pretty strange as we all slept on that communal cell floor and used the same toilet every day. He would only communicate through Abou Monsur; subsequently, when I saw articles about Palestinian attacks, I always wondered whether Kalim was involved. From Abou Monsur we learnt about the prison and who to trust. We were the only Europeans there, except for a Swede who was about forty, but we rarely got to see him. Anyway, he was only there for a few weeks before his release.

If you had to be in prison, this place was the place to be. We had beautiful Lebanese hash to smoke, the guards left you to get on with your lives and that was it. The other prisoners were just doing their time and going home. On the whole, they were all very poor people who had been caught trying to feed their families. People have often said to me that it must have been terrible to be stuck in a foreign prison, but the humanity and kindness there was way beyond anything I was later to experience in British prisons. The only major drawback was that we were a long way from home and we never got any visits, except once when a friend of my brother's, who was travelling, came to see us. Everyone I knew in the business who was doing anything in the Lebanon didn't want to come to the prison, for obvious reasons. However, David had kindly arranged for a carpet dealer he knew to come and drop some money off every few months. The British Embassy came to see us only once the whole time we were there and clearly didn't give a toss whether we lived or died; we were obviously just scum to them.

I never really forgave Steven for giving me up at the airport, although we lived together OK for the duration.

However, we were only to see each other twice after our return. I think he went on to run his father's antiquities business afterwards.

Finally, eighteen months after our bust, the sergeant came and told Steven that he was leaving the next day. I was freaked, as there was no mention of me going. I even started to wonder whether I was ever going to get out of there, but there was nothing I could do about it. The next day Steven was gone and I was left on my own.

The next couple of weeks were dire, as I had no idea whether I was to be allowed to leave or not. Then one day, in July 1970, they came and got me and within a few hours I was on a plane to London with £15 in my pocket.

I sat in that plane looking down on a country I had come to love, even though I had only spent one free night in it. I learnt so much in my time there. The major lesson was that humanity is one. We may look different but underneath, people, no matter where they are from, are the same. Some are bastards and some are great. I made some good friends there and was saved from despair by the kindness of people who had no reason to care about me. I believe that my experiences there determined my attitude of tolerance to others for the rest of my life and I will be forever grateful for the time I spent there. Funny, isn't it, that an experience some would despair of should turn out to be life enhancing?

I thought I would be stopped at customs in London, but I walked straight through. I was so glad to be home. The only trouble was, I had nowhere to go, although I knew from letters that Chris and Jackie were still living in the Brompton Road. I rang from the airport; Jackie answered and told me to go to there.

So it was that I got out of a cab at the corner of Brompton Road and Earls Court Road, outside the flat I had left twenty months before. I'd finally finished up where I'd set out from. It was just that I was rather late and definitely broke.

PART

THE SEVENTIES

CHAPTER SEVEN

IT'S GOOD TO BE BACK

IT WAS GREAT to be home that summer of '70, but I was finding it difficult to readjust. All of my friends were kind to me, but I found myself with no home and no money. In the eighteen months I had been away they had all been busy in one way or another, some for better and some for worse. Myself? Well I was just getting on with it from the day I got back. What else could I do?

Chris and Jackie let me sleep on the sofa in their mansion-block flat in the Brompton Road for the first week, but life felt hard. I wandered around, thrilled at seeing the world as new, but the feeling didn't last, as reality was forever biting at my heels. Besides, the story of my sojourn in Beirut wasn't of much interest to anyone after the first telling. They had lives to get on with and so did I.

I was kindly invited by my old boss at Gear to go and stay at his magnificent country house in Kent the first weekend back and from the moment I left the suburbs I was enthralled by the tones of green. When I got to the house I remember going immediately for a walk in the grounds and then sitting by the moat in awe, taking in the myriad verdant hues that I hadn't seen for so long. It was odd in that I had not thought of such things whilst in the Lebanon, but once I was surrounded by them again I felt a real sense of loss in having been deprived of such beauty for so long.

The house itself was simply stunning and reputed to have been built by the Knights Templar. It seemed lost in time and, in a strange kind of way, it helped me realise that my enforced absence was but a moment in the grand scheme of things and that I really had to get on with a few new plans. It was a lovely break, and fun. Mick Taylor, the Stone who didn't last, was there among a dozen others. Everyone was very kind and we had a good time. That break helped me feel I was coming back into the real world.

On my return to London I was feeling far more positive about the future and got my first lucky break when David asked me to move into his flat in Philimore Gardens. It was a fabulous set-up and within a week or so I was feeling as though I had never been away. David had recently acquired a wonderful sky blue Saab 99 and we bombed around Chelsea in it feeling extremely cool. The best thing of all was that he wanted to take it to Morocco on a carpet-buying trip and kindly asked me to go with him. He really had got his carpet business together by now and was become one of a group of carpet dealers who were to control the business for years – and still do, for all I know.

We thundered down through Europe to Morocco in five days; what a drive that was. Crossing to Ceuta, I remember suggesting we just keep going and head for South Africa. The car was such a joy to drive, you just wanted to go on and on in it. We didn't though.

It was wonderful to be back where it had all started, three long years ago. We went across the Atlas Mountains and down to Goulamein, skirting the Sahara, and it was so beautiful to me to have limitless horizons again after the constrictions of four prison walls. During that trip I came to realise that I had no regrets about my recent experiences; life throws things at you and you make the best of them. I still had my friends, I knew who I was, I had my health and – don't forget – I was still only twenty-one.

I decided on that trip that I didn't want to get into any big scams or involved with more than one or two people if I were to do anything else in the drugs line. I wasn't that money mad, I just wanted enough to make life comfortable. And I was not going to go out chasing something; I would wait and let life come to me.

We spent three weeks in Morocco, had a great time and smoked a lot of kif. We ended up spending a week in Marrakesh because David had fallen in love with a tart in a brothel there. Luckily, the passion wore off, but I didn't mind while it lasted, as the city was then still a marvel of medieval beauty; the grand bazaar was a joy to wander through, or sit in, drinking mint tea and watching the world go by. David was in full Sir Richard Burton mode again, wearing Jellabahs and Moroccan slippers. Mind you, as we weren't doing a scam, so was I.

Finally we headed up to Tangier where David did his serious carpet business with a trader whose shop had a terrace that overlooked the prison courtyard. We threw cigarettes and kif down to some Europeans in the yard. God, that brought Lebanon back; I remember having a tear in my eye when the guys waved and shouted their thanks as they were herded back into the prison. A year later a friend of ours was busted in Tangier, spent eighteen months in that jail and nearly died. He never really got over it.

We did not go up to Ketama from Tangier but spent every evening with Mustapha, the friend who had been our first contact in Morocco. He was doing really well now, with the hordes of hippies coming through. We talked of doing business, but the trouble was that so many people were now being busted with cars and we didn't have a connection for a yacht, which had become the preferred method. David was still getting a commission on anyone he sent – not a lot, but it was handy – and I was to do the same over the next few years. Mustapha always sent the commission in dope via his family – a kilo here, a kilo there – and it came in very handy at times.

We drove back with a car full of rugs and were torn apart when we came back into Dover. Mind you it wasn't really surprising as we were still in Jellabahs and babouches; they must've thought they had a right pair on their hands. Am I glad there are no photos in existence to embarrass me today.

I wasn't really in the mood to be chasing business while I was on that trip. The only chasing I decided on was to find Jane. Jane was the girl I had being going out with for the six months prior to my Afghanistan jaunt. The week before I had left on that fateful trip I had taken a lease on a flat in Fulham and she was to move in while I was away. I was meant to move in on my return from Afghanistan, which of course never happened.

Jane had stopped writing a few months after I had been busted and although I asked Jackie and others about her I got no real answers. I asked David what he knew but he said he'd been pissed off with the way she had dropped me and hadn't bothered to keep in touch with her. He told me I would be a fool to go after her again. Of course, I didn't listen.

Then, one day I was talking to Jackie and she let it slip that Jane had had a bad time with another guy and moved to the country to live with her sister. I asked her to see if she would talk to me and finally she did. Big mistake. They say never go back and I sure shouldn't have. The next five years were hell for both of us, I think. It was no one's fault; in retrospect, it's easy to see the rationale behind it. I'd come back and was looking for someone to relate to. While I had been in prison I had built Jane up in my mind to be a perfect woman, and since she had no one when I came back, we fell into a relationship again.

We were to eventually marry and have a daughter. I won't go into any more details, as she and my daughter have another life now and I do not wish to bring any attention to them. Anyway, before I got back together with Jane, about two months after my return, I was contacted by one of the Chillum brothers who had been released from the Lebanon a few months before me. We got together and talked about doing a switch scam, which was still viable in those days.

It was a very simple scam. Chillum was to score in Pakistan and catch a flight bound for London with a stopover in Zurich. I was to board in Zurich and, on arrival at Heathrow, I would take his bag. If I was stopped by customs, I would say I'd come from Zurich. If they still opened the bag I would be able to say I had picked up the wrong bag. Or so it went in theory.

David very kindly funded the scam for a third of the profit and supplied the contact in Karachi for Chillum to score from. I acquired a passport by the method that was to become well known when used in Forsyth's The Day of the Jackal. And so, three months after my return, I was off to Zurich doing another scam.

Everything went fine, except for the fact that I was stopped by the customs on arrival in Zurich, which was a bit embarrassing because I hardly had anything in the suitcase. Still, it was OK until I returned to the airport the next day to make my rendezvous with the Karachi flight. Then paranoia came bounding in on me and I almost convinced myself that the customs knew who I was and would bust the scam. However, I managed get hold of myself and made it to the lounge, where I saw Chillum sitting waiting for the flight. I'm sure you can guess what he looked like, by the name Chillum. Yep, he was another one like David, who loved dressing native in the British tradition of Burton and T.E. Lawrence and he looked a right prat; especially wearing one of those ridiculous knitted brightly coloured skull caps. Still that would work in my favour, because he would be far more likely to draw customs attention at Heathrow than I was. Mind you, I wasn't exactly dressed in a suit. If I remember rightly, I was rather fond of a cream leather trenchcoat at that time, so I probably thought I was a rock'n'roll manager or something similar. Crazy really, but fronting yourself through customs isn't about looking normal, it's about believing, really believing, that you are not doing anything illegal. It's a knack that you can only discover if you have or not by actually doing it. It's not something you can practise; the problem is, if you haven't got it, it's too late to change your mind once you are stopped.

Anyway, we got back in one piece and even Chillum wasn't stopped, so I was solvent again. With his share of the profit, Chillum went off on the hippie trail to India never to be seen again. I suspect he's sitting in a cave somewhere in Chitral smoking a chillum as I write.

David and I were happy with what we had made and I had enough money to move out of his flat to share a flat in Fulham with another friend. Within a month Jane had moved in and life was really good for a while.

Roly was only living a few streets away and I saw quite a bit of him for a few weeks. He was still the crazy bachelor, but I discovered that he was one of a select band who were getting involved with heroin at the time. I drifted away from him and wasn't to see him again until the early Eighties. By then he was married with three kids and was the squire of the family estate in Suffolk.

Roly's heroin habit was indicative of the big changes in drug consumption that had taken place since my sojourn in Lebanon: the appearance of coke and heroin on a large scale. Before I had left, my friends and I were some of the first people to do coke regularly and even we did not get it all that often. However, in the interim supplies were getting through. Coke was imported by people who liked it. Heroin was imported by businessmen, as the people doing it were too fucked to get it together. The businessmen had seen how the drug experimentation culture had led people to try everything and knew they could make money quickly.

The number of people I was told were doing heroin was astonishing. I had, and have, no interest in heroin at all, and have always found it a weird thing to want to take. However, people whom I've known take it always tell me I don't know what I've been missing. Of course, that shows just how addictive it is: it takes over peoples lives like nothing else.

In fact, heroin becomes the junkie's life; you need it just to be normal. I took coke and smoked dope up until 1987 and I definitely never felt a need to take either every day. For me, they were a recreational thing. Moreover, I have known so many people who have taken those drugs for as long as me, and longer, and they still take them recreationally with no need to fuck themselves up. Naturally, you hear of the crazy ones who just fuck up, but I really can't see how you can blame the drugs; it is the person who is unable to take them. As AA and NA make clear to their members, it is them that is the problem, not the drug concerned.

The reason that governments go on about drugs in such a simplistic way is that if they tried to follow any rational argument they know they would have to concede to legalisation. Also, because they have demonised drugs for political reasons rather than any logical ones, they cannot be seen to do anything other than rant on with their drivel. One just hopes that some day a politician will have the courage to treat the subject intelligently. I won't be holding my breath, though.

Jane and I settled into a fun life hanging out in Chelsea. I lived in the Roebuck, the Water Rat and the Chelsea Potter. David was always about and we did bits of business off and on through to the spring of 1971. I didn't feel ready to do another scam, although I did send others to Morocco and Afghanistan and was paid a commission.

Then, in the spring of 1971, Samir – the translator from the prison in Beirut – was released in the Lebanon and within a couple of months he visited me in London. He took me to Kensington, where I met two Lebanese guys who were shipping beautiful Lebanese Red dope to Europe in drums of olive oil. They were the classic Christian Lebanese, who were schizophrenic in their inability to be either French or Lebanese. They had a food wholesaler in London, to whom they were already shipping the olive oil, but he was having trouble finding outlets as he didn't really want to be involved in the distribution of the dope. These guys had a very safe transport system and had reached the point where it was working like clockwork in Holland and they just needed to sort out the England bit to make it really good. They were sensible: they weren't shipping tons, just 500 kilos every six months – 400 to Holland and 100 to England, where they knew they could earn that bit extra.

I was really keen for this scam, as all I would have to do was arrange to pick up the oil drums every six months, dribble it out at top prices and then pay them three months later when they came to London to bank their money from Holland. Of course, I would work it with David, which made it so easy. The guy who was importing had no need to know who I was, so there was a break between importation and me and as long as I arranged the pick-ups carefully it was a really safe scam. Selling 100 kilos in three months would be no problem and as I had so long, David and I could do it in small 5–10lb deals, and thus charge at the highest prices. It was a lovely scam and worked like a dream. In fact, it was the one scam I was involved in that went quietly and gently. The Lebanese never hassled for their money, the deliveries always came on time and everyone was completely separate from one another, so security was tight. The only trouble was, it stopped after the second one in December '71.

The reason was that the Lebanese guys were involved in a feud in the Lebanon and were shot one day in Baalbek. Samir was OK, as he wasn't part of their family, but was terrified of doing anything after that. I went to Beirut on my false passport in '74 but before we could get a scam going the civil war broke out in 1975. Sadly, Samir had to get out when his family were killed and came to live in London as a refugee. He runs a small hotel now and is as happy as an exile can be although he still has nightmares of that sickening war.

I think that that Lebanese red dope was probably my favourite of all the dopes I have ever had. The Afghani, Nepalese and Chitrali dopes are certainly stronger and trippier, but the Lebanese had a gentle buzz that was delicious. You didn't get completely smashed, it just gave the world a lovely glow. The only comparison I can make is with the effect of natural mescalin compared to that of manufactured LSD.

As for the genetically modified skunk weeds of today, they are beyond belief; THC (tetrahydrocannabinol, the constituent in dope that gets you stoned) gone barmy. I think these skunks are indicative of what has happened to the drug culture over the years, in as much as the pleasure from a drug is now determined by how strong it is rather than the experience enjoyed. Or am I just suffering a druggie's version of that awful disease endemic in Britain, called nostalgia?

CHAPTER EIGHT

ACID DAYS AND THE LAST RESORT: '72 TO '75

AFTER THE SUDDEN discontinuation of the Lebanese scam I was at loss as what to do next. Jane was working in the Kings Road; I was doing nothing and working through my money very quickly. David had gone off to India for six months looking for carpets and I had lost any interest in going off any solo runs.

I think a lot of it was to do with the fact that I now had a wife and felt the need to try and do something normal. I tried to start a business making cowboy shirts with Chris's old partner, Colin. However we weren't that professional about it and I think basically I kept Colin in dope more than anything else, so that petered out and I had even less money.

Chris, being the shrewdie he always has been was doing very well, but was keeping whatever it was that he had going very close to his chest. Which, of course, was fair enough as by this time things had changed markedly from the Sixties. Everyone I knew was very aware of the drugs squad at the time. I never came across them, but they were very active and the looseness about the drugs industry was disappearing rapidly. That group of free-wheeling cops was rampaging around like a bunch of vigilantes, busting some and setting others up to sell drugs for them.

Round about then, I suddenly found myself involved in a completely new line of business. Acid. It was all down to coincidence as usual and definitely nothing planned or looked for. I had taken my share of acid, but for me a trip every six months was about it. Real acid is not a recreational drug, it is something rather more. Some will say it is a religious experience. I wouldn't go that far, but it definitely changes your perception of the world forever and if it's not experienced in the right way it can mess you up. I always think that if people are going to take acid they really need a guide, rather like Carlos Castenada's experiences with mescalin.

As for what people take today called acid, I can't believe that it is the same stuff. The thought that you can be taking real acid every weekend and going out clubbing is just not viable. Real acid cannot be expected to fit in with your social plans; it has its own agenda. I remember one night in the Sixties being invited to The Speakeasy by Percy Raines, who was running the place, and a good friend until he ripped me off many years later. After taking a tab each, Chris, Colin and I went there to see The Moody Blues (I think, but don't quote me on that) and within five minutes of being there we had to get out. Why? Well, once the acid came full on everyone suddenly turned into penguins. This was not a passing fantasy – everyone had turned into walking, talking penguins. I got out of The Speakeasy and felt such relief, all I wanted to do was get home and into bed. When I saw a cab coming down Langham Place from the BBC I knew I was safe and flagged it down. It pulled up and I grabbed the door handle and turned to the driver to say, 'Earls Court Road', then leapt back in horror. Yep. The cab was being driven by a penguin.

I spent the next two hours walking all the backstreets from Oxford Circus to our flat in Earls Court Road so as to avoid any contact with penguins. By the way, I don't have any lasting aversions to penguins.

My whole involvement with dealing acid came about after an Australian named Steve contacted my brother out of the blue, looking for me. Steve was from a wealthy family and had been busted in Beirut with an ounce or two of dope. Somehow he had managed to spend six months in El Ramel prison when I was there and I had given him my brother's address at the time as a contact address.

Steve was an elusive character whom I never really got to know. Later he was to get involved with some weird cult. I think the reason for that was that he had loads of money from his family but no love. The last time I heard from him, in the late Eighties, he invited me to his wedding at the cult's headquarters. I thought I would go along until he added, 'By the way you have to stay for the weekend and our meetings.' I turned down his offer and have never heard from him again.

But that was all in the future. Back in 1972, Steve was the door into a new line of scamming for me. He was a really good-looking guy who had something of the Native American about him. You know those pictures of chiefs in Bury My Heart at Wounded Knee? It was that sort of look. He was now in London and wanted to meet up for a drink. I went to a very nice flat in Islington to meet him and, as far as I was concerned, just to chew the fat. The flat was in one of those beautiful Georgian houses that Tony Blair was to buy later and when I entered it, I walked into

Australia on holiday. It was full of gorgeous Australian girls and surf bum guys, all tanned and rich.

Steve and I said our hellos and went out for a drink. I was in a reverie based on naked Australian girls as we walked down to Camden Passage, when I realised he was talking about acid: 'I don't know if you know anyone but I can move 50,000 tabs a month in Australia if you do.' I had never really thought about selling acid until that moment, simply because it had never come up. I had only bought it for personal use up until that moment.

I was totally up front with Steve. 'To be honest,' I admitted, 'I don't, but I'll see what I can do.' We had a few drinks and talked about guys we had known in Beirut. Then I had to go and meet Jane, who was at Chris and Jackie's flat in the Brompton Road, as we were all going to Thierry's in the Kings Road for dinner. I said my farewells and told him I'd ring in the next few days to let him know how I'd got on.

When I arrived at Chris and Jackie's everyone was ready to go and we went to the Roebuck for a drink before going to eat. Within five minutes the girls were deep in conversation with the wonderfully eccentric and larger-than-life Tommy Roberts, who had the Mr Freedom shop, which then became Malcolm McClaren and Vivienne Westwood's 'Let It Rock', later 'Sex', the home of punk (today it is Westwood's World's End shop). That gave me a chance to have a quiet word with Chris about my conversation with Steve. I was really surprised when he said, 'No problem. I know where we can get as many microdots as we want. The only thing is that they must be for export.'

It was weird. I had shared a flat with Chris and been really close with him for five years and yet he hadn't mentioned a word of this side of himself to me until then. I couldn't work out why and wanted to know more: 'What the fuck? Why haven't you mentioned this before?'

'I'm sorry Bob, but I have to be really careful about this,' he replied. 'The guys who run this are really tight with their organisation and I just didn't think you would know of anyone to sell to abroad until now.'

He was right, of course. Until I had met Steve that day, I knew no one in that line and wouldn't have thought I had any possible outlets abroad prior to that moment. Thus began my involvement with the crew who were to become well known in the infamous Operation Julie acid case of 1977.

Two days after that conversation I went back to see Steve with ten microdots as samples; within a week he had ordered 50,000. To this day I can't figure out where the comparatively small amounts of acid that we sold went, let alone the huge amounts the Julie guys sold in their millions.

Just think about it. From the Sixties through to now, billions – and I mean billions – of tabs of acid have been sold, and where have they all gone? If they are supposed to have been so harmful, why aren't there millions of mental hospitals full of acid victims? Am I being simplistic? I don't know, but it does strange that the world hasn't turned into a mass of tripped-out zombies if acid is so damaging. Then again, the world is run by some pretty weird people. Maybe they are the tripped-out zombies.

To get back to my thing. That first time I scored the acid was £80 per 1,000 tabs and I sold them on to Steve for £100 per 1,000. It was so organised: you ordered what you wanted and when you collected you would be given a bag of shopping and your order would be inside one of the items, such as the cornflakes or the tea; Sainsbury's gone crazy.

The whole thing was simplicity itself. A bag of a thousand would fit easily into your hand, so it was really easy to ship them abroad. Steve was only in London for six months that trip, but he took 50,000 every month, so I made £6,000 in that time. I shared it with Chris, but it was still a very nice little number. I never went out looking for customers for acid, but over the next few years I sent to Australia or Steve collected tabs on a regular basis and there were a few people I knew in the States to whom I sent them when asked.

It was a funny business for me as I wasn't someone who took loads of acid and I never met people who were doing it regularly or anyone it was going to. It ran in a very businesslike manner, and yet acid itself was the last thing you would associate with the word businesslike. Very odd.

The main thing to come out of my involvement with acid wasn't the income, but the fact that it lead to my crazy job for the next four years and a lasting friendship with one of the guys who produced the acid – Eric. Eric is one of life's good guys. We had some good times in the year from '72 to '73. On one memorable occasion, The Grateful Dead came over to play at the Lyceum; Tom, my old boss at Gear, was very close to them and they all came to his house in Chelsea one night. I thought it was so cool and the cruncher of cool was they had this guy with them who had this carpetbag full of drugs. I'm not sure if he was a doctor, but he had a badge from the Federal Drugs Authority that authorised him to carry these drugs legally. Whether it was real or not I don't know, but it was neat. It was a great gig too.

In the Summer of '73, Chris and Eric acquired a restaurant on the Fulham Road that would become the first cocktail bar outside of a hotel in London. It was called the Last Resort, and it was crazy. I would manage it for the next few years and it was such fun. I don't think a night went by without something happening.

Chris designed it and it had a very innovative look, with beautiful marquetry tables in vibrant colours that were rather Peter Max influenced. The walls were black and we even had a wonderful 2-metre-high silver palm tree by Andrew Logan. We also had some wonderful and beautiful waitresses over the years; goodness knows what stories they could tell you.

We opened in late 1973 and it all started that first night, when there were probably more dope dealers in one building at one time than ever before. In fact, I don't think there was anyone there who wasn't involved in drugs in some way. At one point Colin, who as ever was fool in residence, decided to hit everyone who came through the door with amyl nitrate. At that time you could buy it over the counter in chemists. Amyl is a stimulant that is used for heart attack victims and by illegal users as an aphrodisiac, and stinks of rotten socks. The latter always put me off it; it just made my heart go crazy rather than having any really horny effect. Predictably, after Colin's little welcome pop, madness ensued: everyone who came in was given a hit and went into overdrive.

At one point Scotty, who was a roadie with Pink Floyd, had a coke race with Colin. The bar of the Last Resort must have been at least twenty-five feet long and Scotty laid out two lines of coke the full length of it – it must have taken at least an ounce of coke to do it. The two of them then raced to see who could get their line up the quickest.

That was how things were in the Resort from then until it closed in 1979. I never got home before four in the morning, often much later. We would sit in two alcove tables at the back of the basement restaurant for hours talking and getting smashed or head off to somewhere else to party. I drive by its successor now and wonder how the ghosts are doing.

It was a good time, although off and on we would have problems with the local so-called villains, who would come in and act the prat. However, on the whole it was just a good-time bar. The main thing about it was that there was nowhere else like it. We served drinks without food to people we knew, which at that time was illegal, and stayed open late. It sounds crazy now, but then we still had the most stupid licensing laws imaginable, which demanded that you ate when drinking and that everywhere closed early. We were never really harassed by the police; I do remember being raided once, but nothing came of it. The local licensing people didn't like us much, but we simply carried on and the people who used it were cool, so we never had any real problems.

We made a lot of friends with our customers; one who I worked with on a few scams was called Canadian Frank. A complete nutter, he had a thing about handcuffs. I remember going to a flat he was living in Knightsbridge and going into the bedroom for some reason, to be confronted by the sight of his latest girlfriend cuffed to the bed. Voluntarily, I hasten add. And I'll never forget her saying, 'Oh. Hello Bob, you'll have to make your own tea.'

Frank's only comment was: 'She loves it, man.'

He always wore a solid gold belt buckle and some fuck-off diamond rings; he always claimed he wore them in case he had to leg it fast and he would be able to hock them wherever he ended up. I tend to think it was more him being a bit flash. Always cool, though.

I tended to drift away from scamming while I was married and working at the Resort. I would do the odd deal around town but no travels as such. David would still got off on his journeys, come into the Resort and make me green with envy, but by now Jane and I had a child, so domesticity and safety came first. I was having a reasonably good time and was paid well, and that was my life for a few years.

Mind you, talking of safety … My wife was going to see Chris and Jackie one evening while I was working and I went with her to the flat in the Brompton Road; Chris wasn't there. Jane and I were sitting and having a chat when the bloody door came crashing in and the place was suddenly being raided by the customs. It was mayhem for a couple of minutes. Anyway, things settled down and then they searched the place while Chris and Jackie's daughter cried. The customs asked who we were but when I gave my name there was no reaction, so I clearly wasn't on their list that day. After a search and finding nothing, that was it – they were gone.

I went off to work and as I got to the junction of the Fulham Road and Redcliffe Gardens, I saw Chris in his Beetle and shouted for him to stop. I went over.

'Have you been home?'

'No. Why?' He asked.

'You've just been busted,' I told him.

'Shit! Did they find anything?'

'No.'

'Well, that was lucky. There's 5,000 tabs in the head of a teddy bear pyjama case,' he said smiling, before calmly driving off. I couldn't believe what I'd just heard. I had seen a customs guy put his hand inside that pyjama case. Thank God he didn't feel up inside the head.

In retrospect, that time seems to have come and gone so quickly and all those nights in the Last Resort seem to meld into one long night. Which probably isn't that far from the truth.

Things changed with the break up of my marriage, though and I was back on my travels. Although, at first, that meant just a short hop across the water to Amsterdam.

CHAPTER NINE

MICK, NELSON
AND LEN

MICK IS A short guy with an almost Romany face, eyes like daggers and lots of tattoos. His eyes have a way of burning into people and if he is fired up – which is most of the time – they can cut them in two. He is a classic example of the short guy with a need to prove himself and made a habit of provoking situations just for the hell of it. It could be very trying at times. If you had to compare him to an animal, Mick is a Jack Russell terrier. He can go berserk at the smallest thing. He would worry and harass you to your wits' end at the drop of a hat and yet, like a Jack Russell, he could be a lovely, gentle friend. A contradiction and mystery he certainly is, and crazy without a shadow of a doubt.

He had been living in Amsterdam for two years after a deal had gone wrong in London – he just managed to get out of the back door over the garden fence and away as the cops were literally coming through the front door. Close shave. He always claimed to have seen some fat cop puffing and struggling to get over the fence as he ran. Apocryphal maybe, but a nice image.

Mick was one of those people who lived in a pit. I don't know how he did it – maybe he doesn't any more – but muck and mess followed him then. It was horrific. I guess it was partly due to the fact that he always had a menagerie around him. A minimum of two dogs (yes, usually Jack Russells), cats, the odd cockatoo and maybe a snake or two. I think the truth is, he loved animals more than people. He wasn't the easiest of people to get on with, as he had an awful temper and was hard to handle at times.

I think he knew he was hard work and found it easier to relate to animals than to people.

The most painful animal in residence in the Amsterdam flat was the bloody cockatoo called Nelson. He was allowed to roam and had a nasty habit of picking on people when they were least expecting it. One of his favourite tricks was to flap into the loo and try and bite your willy when you were having a pee. You soon learnt to sit down for a pee in that flat.

I had decided to go over and see Mick after the break-up of my marriage. So I took some time off from the Last Resort and nipped over for the weekend. Amsterdam was and is, as we all know, a place where you can enjoy getting stoned without feeling paranoid. Mick enjoyed this freedom to the full and then some. He was living in one of those flats up a million stairs overlooking a canal. It was lovely to sit there of an evening, smoking a joint and watching the world go by – if the animals would let you. The only trouble besides the animals was that the flat had a continual flow of visitors and was more like Schipol check-in than a flat. So the chances of enjoying the view in peace were rare.

The day I arrived coincided with a no-visitors evening, though, and Nelson was asleep on his perch, so Mick and I sat smoking joints, having the odd line of coke and talking. I was pretty depressed following the break-up of my marriage and although I had been having a good time running the Last Resort, I had not made any real money for a few years. I told Mick I was single now and had the time and inclination to get down to some serious business. He was up for it as he had done several scams to England but the people he had worked with had always paid late and short and this had left him struggling for money as well.

We decided that we would start a coke scam, with me running a couple of kilos as a body pack every month or so. We would make about £10,000 between us on every trip. The only trouble was that coke was difficult to come by on credit and we had no money. However, Mick had a Dutch friend, Jaan, who had promised him up to a 100 kilos of dope on tick as he was having a tough time. We figured we would make enough money after doing two trips of the dope to start the coke scam. The reason for opting for a coke scam was that we wouldn't have the overheads involved with shipping bulky dope, i.e. you have to pay the transportation fees and, more importantly, it involves more people, which increases the chances of someone fucking up besides having to pay them.

Mick had a meeting arranged with Jaan the next day so we spent the rest of that evening hanging out in the red-light district, which was only a ten-minute walk from his place. I shiver to think about it, even now. Mick was a maniac and the night ended with us heading back to the flat with about twenty people and I didn't got to bed until 10 a.m. I woke screaming from a nightmare in which I'd been the victim of an avian attack straight out of Hitchcock's The Birds. The trouble was, it wasn't a dream. I had Nelson hanging on to my upper arm and blood was streaming down it.

Mick came in and tried to prise the bird from my arm. Then the phone rang and Mick left me fighting with the damn thing to answer it.

'Keep quiet!' he shouted at me, as I screamed when the beak went in another inch. 'We'll be there in ten minutes,' he said into the phone, as I finally prised Nelson's beak from my arm and he flew squawking in victory to the lampshade. I could still hear the bastard screaming his pleasure at having had some flesh as we got into Mick's BMW and roared off to the Yacht Club. I should have known it was going to be one of those evenings.

I had slept all day, which I hate doing, had the hangover from hell, my arm was sore and Mick was driving like a bloody maniac. Some cool and groovy weekend this was turning out to be. The only groove I had was the one in my arm from the bird's beak.

We arrived at the club in five minutes flat. Mick was out of the car and into the club before I'd even closed my door. I entered the club to see Mick at the bar talking nineteen to the dozen. I walked to the bar, nodded a hello to Jaan and, while rubbing my injury, proceeded to down two beers in rapid succession in an attempt to anaesthetise both my arm and brain – with minimal effect.

Jaan, the guy Mick was so deep in conversation with, was a friend of his who was a serious player in the Amsterdam dope scene. Everyone knows how liberal the Dutch are with regard to possession, but they do give out prison sentences for trafficking – although they are rarely for terms of more than six years and everyone seems to go home at weekends. Jaan had recently finished a short sentence for 100 kilos of dope and was intent on getting in front again.

'I can pick it up any time,' he was saying.

'Right, I'll meet you next Tuesday,' Mick told him. 'What time?'

'I'll be there for 2 p.m.'

'OK. I'll come on my own and you too. I really don't want to be mob handed,' Mick explained. 'It's so much easier if it's just us.'

I was pleased to hear this, as I really didn't want to be with Mick when the business was done as he was always like a jack in the box. He would drive around for ages before going to a meet, checking to see whether he was being followed but driving so fast that I always thought he would draw attention to himself even if he wasn't initially being followed.

Mick was already into his third large bourbon and coke and we'd only been there fifteen minutes. He was trying to get Jaan to stay, but the Dutchman was making his apologies and on his way in seconds. He gave me a knowing smile and nod as he headed for the door. He was no fool!

Mick turned to me while I rubbed the huge bruise that was coming up where Nelson had grabbed me and asked what I fancied doing that night. I knew he was up for it. We had just missed the whole of Saturday and here we were off again. Christ, I never learnt. I excused it by saying I was single again and so another night went by in a haze of sex, drugs and rock and roll.

I was awoken abruptly at lunchtime Sunday to see the beautiful American girl with whom I had ended the night getting dressed and shouting, 'Can't you stop that thing?' Yep, Nelson was trying to break the door down to eat my flesh again. I struggled out of bed, knowing there was no chance of morning-after sex, grabbed a towel, flung the door open and threw the towel over the damn bird. As I struggled with my nemesis, the gorgeous American's very cute arse wiggled through the door and was gone.

I could have quite happily killed Nelson at that moment, but the bugger escaped the towel and was up on the lampshade. I went back to my room with the sound of his guffawing victory going through my brain like a jackhammer.

After lunch, Mick drove me to Schipol. While I listed various sadistic methods of killing Nelson, I did briefly mention I would ring on Thursday to confirm we were on for the scam.

I returned to London and work, so the week flew by. I went to see David, who agreed to lend me a Transit he had that had a false floor, on the condition that he got to sell the dope, which was fine with me. I arranged to pick up some of Mick's furniture from his ex-wife on the Saturday to take over. As shipping furniture was to be the cover on the way out and on the return trip, I was to bring back some rural Dutch furniture.

I rang Mick on the Friday and we were on. So I was on the ferry Saturday and arrived in Amsterdam in the early hours of Sunday morning. I rang the bell to the flat and

Mick let me into bedlam. It was three in the morning and the flat was full of people. They were all out to lunch and of course muggins here, who was knackered and only wanted to go to bed, got stuck into the coke. The next thing I knew it was 10 a.m. and bedtime with a woman I didn't know – and no, it wasn't the American with the divine arse.

I was awoken by Mick shaking me at five in the afternoon; he was going potty. After fighting my way back into consciousness I realised that he was going mad about Nelson being ill. The damned bird was squawking like a banshee, which was doing nothing for my hangover and I could have quite easily cooked him. Still, I struggled out of bed, got dressed and made sense of Mick saying we had to get to a vet as the bird had eaten a packet of coke. Christ that was all I needed, a wired cockatoo.

We managed to get the bloody thing into an orange box and into the back of the Transit, which I'd parked outside. Then we headed off towards an emergency vet with the muffled squawks jamming my ears along with an intermittent sawing noise. The next thing I knew was that the damn bird was flapping and screaming around my head as I drove. I ran across a traffic island being so distracted and hungover and came to a halt about three feet from a canal.

I jumped out, slamming the door, and sat with my head in my hands, looking into the canal with a headache that ran around my head like a steel band and into my eyes via red hot pokers, thinking, 'What the fuck?' Mick finally got

Nelson into a blanket I had in the transit and when I opened the back door I saw how the damn thing must have escaped. The intermittent sawing I had heard was him working through the lid of the orange box, using his beak like a chainsaw in overdrive because he was so wired. A cop came over to see what we were up to; he went into hysterics when he heard what had happened and told us to get on to the vet.

The moral of this tale is, don't leave coke lying around if you've got a cockatoo. Even better, don't own a cockatoo. (For the benefit of any cockatoo lovers who may be reading this, Nelson recovered.)

No more excitement occurred before Mick came back from the pickup on the Tuesday. We shoved the dope in the transit, closed the back doors lifted the floor panel and stashed it. We then loaded in a few pieces of Dutch furniture and I was off to Dieppe.

I was fine about doing this run. Well, I say that, but we didn't really have any choice, as we had no money to pay someone else to do it. Of course, we used Dieppe as that way I wouldn't have to declare I'd been in Holland at customs. Just for cover, Mick had got a false invoice printed for the furniture using the name of a shop in Ghent that he knew of. We figured that the customs would be satisfied with this if they bothered to stop me and unless I got one of their random strip-downs, where they take a vehicle apart, everything would be fine.

Sure enough, they didn't stop me at either customs and by the following weekend David had settled up and I flew to the Dam and paid Mick on the Sunday. We decided to leave it for a month before doing the second one. So I flew back to London that day and was back running the Last Resort on the Monday.

* * *

The month was up before I knew it. Mick rang me one Monday and said he'd arranged to pick-up the following Monday so, could I get the Transit and come over at the weekend. I went to see David to borrow the Transit again as I had arranged when he had paid me off for the last run. However I was in for a shock. David in his wisdom had sent the van off to Spain to pick up some dope of his own, so I was fucked. However, David came up with a solution of sorts.

He said he had seen an old friend of ours the week before named Len, who was struggling and was looking to earn some money. We had known Len for five or six years. He never sold dope, but he was a great driver and worked for various people. We got to know him when he was running backwards and forwards to Switzerland on a coke scam. He never got stopped, as you would never in a million years think of him as being involved with anything nefarious.

He was a guy of about fifty and looked like the archetypal bank clerk. Thin, wiry body, average height with a long, sad, skeletal face, hardly any hair and a voice that never went above a whisper. To complete the stereotype, he wore thick glasses and wore the best polyester. It was not an affected image – this was simply how he was. The only thing that distinguished Len from a bank clerk was that he was a complete nutter. He not only thrived on danger, he went looking for it.

David told me he would do the run for 5 kilos and, as I had no other courier, I rang Mick and put it to him. He laughed when I told him the method, but was up for it – he was as desperate as I was to get on to our coke scam.

I rang Len and he came down from his home in near Colchester. We had a drink at Liverpool Street and talked it through. I wasn't that happy with his means of transport, but he was really confident and said it had worked three times before. So, without being super-optimistic, I arranged to meet him in Rotterdam the following week.

I flew out to Amsterdam on the Monday and Mick already had the dope. The following morning we drove up to Rotterdam. Len had caught the overnight ferry; we rang him at his hotel at 9 a.m. and we were off by 9.30, Mick and I in his BMW following Len and his brother in their white Transit out of town and towards the coast. I still don't know where we ended up exactly. It was a quiet river estuary and we could see the sea about a mile away. That was all I could make out. All I wanted to do now was to unload and get out of there.

We pulled up at the top of a dyke, where a heron sat and watched us with a mournful air. Len and his brother pulled a deflated Zodiac dinghy from the back of the Transit, started up a small compressor and rapidly inflated the Zodiac, which we all carried down to the water. Then we brought down a big outboard motor, fitted it and loaded two cans of fuel. We brought down the dope and roped it down in the dinghy. Len's brother nipped back to the van and came down with a rucksack containing whatever Len needed for the journey. And that was it. He was off. 'I'll see you later,' he shouted as he pulled away and shot down the estuary.

I thought we would never see him again. I still can't believe that anyone would willingly cross the North Sea in an inflatable dinghy, but Len did. What's more, I still can't believe that I was desperate enough to entrust a scam to a rubber dinghy.

We watched until he was out into the open sea. Mick and I shared a look and a shrug, which summed up how mad we were to expect this to work. With not a word said he got into his car and I got into the Transit with Len's brother to head for the ferry and Harwich.

Most of the trip back I was looking across the North Sea for an inflatable – with no luck – or looking at the sky, praying it would stay clear. We were back in Harwich so quickly I couldn't believe it. I had been so caught up in worrying about Len that the time had flown by. The one thing that repeatedly came to my mind was the thought of Len drowning. I kept getting an image of his glasses spiralling down into that that cold, grey sea.

We were out of Harwich and back to the place that Len and his brother owned in no time. The house was at the end of a lane and backed on to an estuary with a jetty. It was a real tip, surrounded by dead cars and sundry junk. Surrounded by swamp and mud with the tide out, I couldn't help but think of Magwich escaping from the prison hulks on the Thames in David Copperfield. The sun was shining, which gave an eerie beauty to the scene, but there was always the underlying awareness of the harshness of nature in the blinding glare of the sun reflecting from the mud. Still, it was quiet and isolated and we sat looking out through the filthy window that looked out on to the river and down towards the sea praying for Len to appear sooner rather than later.

It was early evening by now. We had been tied up in this all day; by now, the adrenaline was wearing out and tetchiness was creeping in. Len's brother and I took it in turns to keep our eyes on the estuary for the next few hours, but saw nothing.

We strained our eyes harder and harder as the grey of the evening turned to a pitch-black night. The only good thing about this was that if we couldn't see Len, no one else would be able to either. I had absolutely no idea of how Len was navigating in the Stygian darkness and I didn't feel like asking his brother, as I dreaded hearing him say that he didn't know. We had seen nothing on the river since sunset and had only heard the occasional puttering of an engine in the distance, which got our hopes up only to dash them as the sound died.

Around one o'clock in the morning we were stirred from our dozing by the sound of an outboard – and it wasn't moving away. It was coming closer by the second.

We were up and out and staring into the darkness and then suddenly Len was there.

I felt so happy. In his quiet way, Len simply tied the dinghy up, clambered out and walked wearily towards the house. His brother and I quickly got the dope out of the dinghy and got it into the Transit and covered.

We went back into the house and found Len fast asleep on the sofa, still in waterproofs and wellies. I left him the agreed 5 kilos as the fee and his brother kindly drove me and the dope back to town.

David had sold the lot by the following evening and we had settled up with Jaan within five days. So everyone was happy. Mick and I had made £20,000 a piece; we were ready to roll with the coke scam.

I decided not to do it that week and thought I'd go back via Harwich and see Len, as he might want to carry on with the crazy Zodiac scam. So I came back via Harwich and rang him to go out for a drink. His brother answered the phone and said Len had died the night before of a heart attack. I felt as though I had been hit with a hammer. One minute I was enjoying the taste of success only for it to turn to ashes in my mouth the next.

In my dreams I still see Len lying in his wellies and waterproofs, fast asleep. A nice guy gone and I can't find fault with his life; he was honest, did his thing and was absolutely fearless.

CHAPTER TEN

TROUBLE IN PARADISE

MICK AND I were able to score coke from some Colombians he knew in the Dam for £12,000 per kilo. I would knock it out for £800 an ounce, thereby returning £28,000 per kilo. It took three months to sell 2 kilos, but we were happy with that. We had no overheads and no one else was involved except the three people I sold to. I had known these three for years and there were no problems with them at all. I would fly to Brussels or Paris, catch the train up to the Dam and spend a few days with Mick. Then I'd strap on the 2 kilos, which was really easy, jump on the train back to whichever city I'd flown into and return to London. I never got stopped; life was good.

I stopped running the Last Resort in the Spring of 1976, after the second scam. We worked the scam for about two years, from the summer of 1976 until 1979, doing eight runs altogether, so we made £128,000 less expenses on paper. However, things aren't like that, or not for me anyway. I enjoyed my life. I was single and London was fun. It's funny, the way the Seventies are written about now you would think it a was dire and crass decade. Well, I didn't think so. I was out every night and it was great. The only difference was that the drug of choice now was coke, not dope. This led to not going to bed before dawn, sleeping until lunchtime and then starting again. Not every day, but a few days a week. I'd stopped working, so I was free to do what I wanted and I spent much of my time going on holiday. During this period I spent a lot of time in the Greek islands, which I love to this day, even if they are getting a bit too popular for my liking.

The problem was that I went everywhere on my own. It became a very solitary time for me. It's funny, that whole mythology about the idea that when you have coke around you a lot you are never without women. Well it's true, but the only problem is that the coke becomes the primary focus, so it's not the greatest pulling magnet of all time. Also, it becomes very expensive, as before you know it you are laying out maybe 7 grammes a night. Of course, at the time you're Mr Generous and don't give a fuck. Then again, maybe it's just me and I didn't have the desire to pull on the strength of laying out lines, which always seemed a seedy idea to me anyway.

I was off on my travels to wherever between my trips to see Mick. I was never really close to him, we were just business associates. I didn't enjoy the way he would always be getting out of it, noisy and drawing attention to himself. I liked a quiet life, on the surface at least.

While I was in London I spent a lot of time with David, who was doing very well as a carpet dealer by this time. He was still as outrageous as ever but in a very civilised way. On one occasion we went to Clonakilty in Ireland, where he had thought about setting up home at one point, and I really don't know how we came away alive. The Irish propensity for consuming gallons of alcohol freaked me totally. I could only keep up by tooting a lot of coke. To this day I can't work how they can stay standing with no drugs to counterbalance the alcohol. Every night we swore we would get an early night and every bloody night we ended up smashed to bits by 3 a.m. One time, David met some

Dutch guy who was touring the area and we ended up sitting up all night discussing the idea of growing weed in the area as it is extremely mild, being in the Gulf Stream. We then spent the next week driving round looking at any house that had a walled vegetable garden or large greenhouse. Forget the house – we went straight out to the gardens. I think the agents must have thought we were mad. Of course, nothing came of it at the time.

Being involved with coke such a lot of the time led to a lot of partying and I seemed to drift away from my old dope-dealing pals. I would occasionally see them, but they seemed to have headed out to the country, whereas I was totally into city life. I was also spending money fast and furiously and I never bothered to buy an apartment, which must be one of my most stupid mistakes. I was always saying I'd do it tomorrow, and of course tomorrow never came. I won't say I was a lost soul, but I was definitely going nowhere, simply doing my trips to the Dam and then spending and going on holiday.

This changed after one evening in February '78, when Mick and I were dining out before I flew back to London on my seventh trip. We were having a quiet satay in town and had nearly finished dinner when Mick leant across the table and said, 'I've got a really good one for us in Jamaica. You know Thomas, who I scored the last 2 kilos from? Well, he said he would turn us on to his guy in Jamaica if we bring him back a kilo at cost plus a £3,000 fee for turning us on to the connection. So I was thinking, when we've done this we could go and have a holiday and do that. I know you've got that guy who can make the camera cases. What do you think?'

In fact, I had already had one camera case made up. It was aluminium, with a false bottom in which you could fit about 4 kilos of coke. I had it made by a friend, as I had started to put together a scam out of Rio with a crazy guy I had known a year before, but it had come to nothing after he had gone off to Rio to set it up. I wasn't to hear from him for three years, but that's another, freaky, story. I knew that my mate could make a case for Mick in a couple of days if I paid him £100.

Sitting in the restaurant that cold and wet evening in February, Jamaica seemed a very good idea indeed. So without too much thought, I said yes. Mick told me of a house in Runaway Bay a friend of his owned that he had already sussed was available. We agreed to rent it for three weeks, so all we had to do was confirm the dates, get the tickets and go.

Two weeks later (the first week of March 1978, to be precise) we were cruising through a midday tropical shower on our way to Montego Bay in our hired Lada to meet Hector. We were having a great time smoking some very funky weed I had bought from a Rasta on the beach by the Runaway Bay golf club – which doesn't have a golf course, but what the hell. We were following a beat-up old Mercedes with a TV on the back shelf. I worked out that it was positioned so the driver could see what was on TV. That's Jamaica for you.

Jamaica is wonderfully surreal for an Englishman. Driving through villages named for English villages, you sometimes imagine you're in Devon because the countryside is so verdant and a cow is on the green, but then you look again and there's a gaudy parrot (but thank God no bloody cockatoos) amidst some stunning tropical flowers and beyond, the blue, blue Caribbean – which could never be mistaken for the Atlantic.

Hector was a complete unknown to me, but Mick had known Thomas for several years and had been scoring coke from him for our last two scams. So we felt as relaxed as we could be under the circumstances.

We went to Tryall, the trendy resort just outside of Montego Bay, as we had arranged over the phone before we left Europe. It is horrendous. It was once a sugar planters' home and it sits languidly on a hill looking out across the Caribbean, but it is ruined by its fake colonial style and the naffness of rouched curtains and gold taps. The clientele treated the staff as if they were still slaves, which I found disconcerting.

After we had had a couple of rum punches on the terrace, watching American tourists behave like shits, Hector turned up, late by European standards but on time by Jamaican ones. Hector was black and big; he was of an ebony hue, so deep and dark that it turned gunmetal blue in certain lights. He had a bald head and shades and starting from his neck he was as solid as rock – and a big rock at that, as he was about 6 feet tall. He didn't exude menace, just hardness. I was glad when he said he didn't want a drink and he suggested we leave. As he turned to leave, I saw a livid grey scar running across the back of his neck and I realised that this guy was not just tough, he was the epitome of tough.

We drove back round the headland, feeling good simply wallowing in the warmth and beauty, into Montego Bay itself, then into a slum. Our white faces were regarded menacingly by everyone as we drove through and as the roads were so chock full of people we moved slowly, which made the menace seem to hang even more heavily. It made for a distinctly uncomfortable ride, but once the onlookers saw who we were with, they carried on with their business.

I was annoyed, as I didn't want to be seen as yet another honky, but that's the way it was and there was nothing I could do about it. We ended up in a rum shack that had a definite ring of the cowboy bar about it – except for the thumping reggae, that is. Hector lead us through the back into the yard, which was full of rubbish from the bar and a line with washing flapping on it. We sat down under the shade of a corrugated roof amidst crates and empties and got down to business.

It was all very simple. Hector could get us whatever we wanted within a day and the price was $10,000 a kilo. A kilo is 35 ounces and in England an ounce would sell for £800. The exchange rate back then was about $1.80 to the pound, so the cost was approximately £5,250 per kilo; therefore, the returns were good. On a kilo, if you sold it in ounces, the return would be approximately £30,000 before expenses. This was seriously good money. Even if you sold it as a single kilo you could expect £25,000, so you would still clear about £18,000 to £19,000 on each one.

Mick and I had decided to buy just 1 kilo apiece, plus the kilo for Thomas on this first trip. We were being careful, as we didn't know Hector personally. He was very cool and he seemed genuine, but how were we to be certain? We sat and drank rum and smoked some weed for an hour or so and when we asked for a sample of the coke he disappeared into the bar and returned with a small plastic bag containing a single crystal that must have weighed about two grammes. It was good, clean coke, probably Colombian. If the kilos were as good, we were on to a winner. We arranged to meet Hector two days later in the market at Ochos Rios, where he had a stall, to confirm if we wanted to score on not.

Hector sent one of his posse from the bar with us to make sure we got out of the area safely and within ten minutes we were back on the road to Runaway Bay in the afternoon sunshine, skimming along the edge of the ocean. Stoned on rum and dope listening to some great reggae on the tinny radio. Life was good.

We got back to the house and spent the next twelve hours getting smashed and having a great time. I didn't feel particularly good the next day when I got up about lunchtime, but it wasn't that painful. After all, I was in Jamaica. The pool washed the pain away and life felt good.

Mick and I decided that we would go ahead with the deal. The only problem would be where we would do the trade, as we didn't want to be somewhere closed in and we didn't want Hector coming to the house. There was a small supermarket just outside town and we thought we would do the deal there as it was relatively open and yet we could be seen stopping with no problems.

The next day, after going to the beautiful Dunns River Falls, we went on into Ochos Rios. It was no more than a village back then, with a few shops and the harbour with a bauxite pier, which was completely out of context in such idyllic surroundings. Still, it was a gentle town and we wandered around quite happily, spending time in the beautiful gardens above the town. Then we walked around looking at the T-shirts and terrible carvings, Jamaica's answer to Spanish bulls. Who buys those things? We saw Hector chatting up some American girls and waited until they moved on before going over and saying hello. He was in a good mood, having arranged to meet the girls that evening. We went to a bar in the town and arranged to do the business the following lunchtime. Hector was fine about doing the switch at the supermarket. We agreed to meet first at the Runaway Bay golf club, where we would show him the money. Then one of us would go with him to see the coke and we would meet at the supermarket and do the switch.

Mick and I were really enjoying ourselves. It was so relaxing and everyone we met was so friendly, barring our experience in the slum of Montego Bay. We were invited to a reggae concert up in the hills that night and we had a great time there. The concert was set up in a natural amphitheatre, the only light coming from the stage and a full moon shining through the lianna and trees. It was beautiful; the rum, joints and West Indian food cooked on open fires added to a truly memorable night. We were the only white people there, but there were no bad vibes; we got stoned and danced to some fabulous reggae and weren't hassled when we danced with some local girls. Mind you, our dancing definitely deserved the occasional snigger; although we thought we could dance, we had nothing on the locals. We finally managed to drive home through the twisting lanes at about three in the morning, singing, laughing and feeling fine. Then, to complete our joy, we saw the Caribbean fringed with palms, glinting below us in the spectral white moonlight. Life was complete at that moment; Mr Happy was in his element.

The following morning, we were still buzzing from our night in the hills and we spent it sunbathing and swimming in the house pool. The women who looked after us cooked us pancakes, which we ate sitting by the pool. We knew this was the start of a beautiful friendship and we plotted how we were going to set up home in Jamaica and run 20 kilos a month out during the holiday season. We decided that we would be back within weeks and looked forward to talking about the logistics with Hector at lunchtime.

We put the $30,000 in a beach bag, put a towel over it and made the two-minute drive to the golf club. The club was very Jamaican, in that it didn't have a golf course and was in fact a beach bar. We sat on the lawn with the sea blue and sparkling ten yards away. The beach had a few people on it. I waved hello to the guy who had the weed franchise and we settled down with rum punches to wait for Hector.

He arrived a half hour later, when we were on our second drinks. He was accompanied by a guy who was even bigger than him and wore a white capped-sleeve T-shirt that made his arms look like tree trunks. I figured he could crush you to death with just one of those arms.

We sat and chatted about our idea for coming back and Hector was all for it. He said he would be able to find us a house and that there would be no problem with supply as it was coming through all the time on its way to the States. After ten minutes of chatting, Mick pushed the beach bag next to Hector, who picked it up, put it on his lap and had a look at the notes. He didn't physically count it – no one ever does in such circumstances. It's just that you know amounts after handling cash so regularly. Hector did pull a couple of the hundred dollar bills out, slipped them into his pocket and said he was going to the toilet. He did this so as to check they weren't counterfeits. He came back after a couple of minutes and said everything was fine.

We agreed that Mick would stay with the incredible hulk and the money while I went for a drive with Hector to check the 3 kilos of coke. The two of us wandered over to Hector's jeep, which was parked in the shade and roared off. Hector told me to grab an ice box that was behind my seat. The coke was kept in the ice box to avoid the high humidity, which can lead to it becoming hydroscopic – that is, it will absorb moisture and become unstable and end up as rubbish, not a good idea. I opened the box and there were what looked like – as far as I could estimate – three kilo blocks of very fine flake cocaine. I opened one of the bags and put a little on my tongue and it tasted as it should. Then I sniffed the bag. It had that distinctive cat's piss aroma that some good cokes have. I was satisfied and told Hector we should pick up the others and do the trade.

It only took ten minutes and we were back at the bar. Hector pulled up and beeped and the others came out to join us. The giant got in with Hector and I walked over and joined Mick in our car. Mick drove and we followed Hector to the supermarket. As we drove up I realised that it was closed for the afternoon siesta and there was no one there, but I wasn't too bothered, as everything had flowed so easily so far. That was a mistake.

The supermarket was on the road with a car park at the front and an alley that ran round the back. Hector drove round the back; we presumed he wanted to do the swap out of sight. Mick swung round in the car park so as to be facing the road so that we could get away quickly. I got out with the bag and sauntered around the back of the supermarket, past some stinking bins full of what smelt like rotting fish and as I reached the corner I gagged on the smell and lurched forward.

That lurch saved my life. As I lurched forward a machete whistled across the top of my head and thunked into the wooden panelling of the supermarket. I looked up and there was the fucking hulk trying to pull it out. I don't know how, but I shot up and because he was unbalanced trying to pull the machete from the panelling I knocked him flat on his back.

As he fell, I saw Hector leaping from the jeep fifteen yards away with another machete. I turned and ran. Mick saw me coming with Hector screaming behind me, his machete raised. I dived into the Lada and screamed for Mick to drive. The next second Hector swung his machete at the window, which smashed, but as I had the beach bag in my hands it lodged in it and then we were gone. The Lada didn't exactly shoot away, but at least it went. Hector was left standing and we had a free machete lodged in the bag.

Mick drove like the clappers towards the house; we didn't say a word. After five minutes it looked as if we were safe as there was no sign of Hector and the hulk following us. Until then I had been so caught up in the adrenaline rush of getting away that I was aware of nothing, but at that point I started shaking and, glancing down, noticed I had wet shorts where I had pissed myself. Through the mist of adrenaline I became conscious of Mick shouting, 'I'll kill the cunt!'

It didn't matter. We had got away, that was all that I cared about, and now we had to get out of Jamaica. Fast, if you don't mind! I realised I had gone from love to hate in minutes. Ten minutes before I wanted to stay in Jamaica forever; now I was desperate for England and the rain.

Neither Mick nor I had told Hector where we were staying, but Runaway Bay was not that big a village at that time. Consequently, we were very nervous as we drove to the house, but there was no sign of him when we arrived. We went in, grabbed our bags and were gone in five minutes flat. Alas, we didn't even see the lovely ladies who had looked after us, as we were in and out so quickly. Within forty-eight hours, I was in London and Mick was in Amsterdam.

I was so pissed about what had happened. I couldn't work out why Hector wanted to rip us off. It could have been the start of a really good business relationship, but he just had his mind set on ripping us for $30,000. Forget the fact that he was willing to kill for it. I still can't believe that he'd do such a thing; it is impossible to comprehend that sort of thinking. You might say that is the way things work over there, and it's true to a certain extent. My experiences in the Caribbean and South America confirm that these cultures have a lack of respect for human life that is totally outside our social norms. In that line of work, and in those places, it is truly dog eat dog and you are in trouble if you think otherwise.

Mick was raving mad for weeks afterwards and attacked Thomas, the guy who had turned us on to Hector, one night in a club in Amsterdam. However, it achieved nothing. I suppose Hector was either doing bigger business with the guy or maybe the guy was dealing with someone further up the chain and had never come into contact with Hector. There was nothing we could do about it anyway, that was for sure. We just had to put it down to experience.

The final piss off was that I really loved Jamaica but I've never been able to go back since. I sometimes feel that machete swishing over my head in my dreams and wake up sweating.

PART
③

THE
EIGHTIES

CHAPTER ELEVEN

COCI THE
CHEMIST

I HAVE NEVER felt any need to apologise for what I've been involved in, as it is part of the life and society I live in. I don't know anyone who is vehemently anti-dope or coke. Yes, people have a down on smack but that is more to do with the perception that it is so destructive. I read the press on drugs and it baffles me, because I know an awful lot of media people, and the vast majority, if not all, take drugs themselves. It is as if they write one thing and live another; double standards rule. I, and a lot of the people I know, have been taking drugs now for up to thirty-five years and believe me, we are not fucked up. Of course, I have come across the odd casualty who crashed because of drugs, but certainly nowhere near the number who have been destroyed through alcohol abuse.

I understand the concern of politicians that people may fuck themselves up by taking drugs. After all, that was the reason for the first drugs laws – everyone was getting smashed on laudanum. I am not even sure I am in favour of total decriminalisation. However, people seem to have a innate drive to get out of it on drugs, whether they be legal or illegal. There is a very interesting book – The Alchemy of Culture, by R. Rudgley – that suggests we have a genetic predisposition for the escape drugs provide. This argument seems extremely coherent to me when you consider that humans have been getting out of it for millennia. Only a hundred years ago, taking drugs was commonplace. Queen Victoria, Gladstone and many other eminent Victorians took cocaine and laudanum and yet no one says they were incapable of carrying out their official duties.

I find it so ridiculous that governments refuse to accept that humanity has been taking mind-bending drugs since the year dot. They seem to think that if they refuse to discuss the subject coherently it will go away, which is patently absurd. I'm not saying that we would all be better human beings if we were legally allowed to take drugs, but it seems even to me that governments worldwide aren't going to achieve anything with their present policies, such as they are. If the British government, for example, would only consider the idea of selling drugs legally, they could control and monitor the situation and tax it. If there is such a problem with drugs, the tax income could be used to deal with the health problems instead of going into other's pockets.

The question is, why does society make such a big deal out of drugs? Is it that it's a scapegoat for society's ills? I don't know. It seems really weird to me, though, that there is no dialogue about these things. Or is it that it is something that we cannot talk about in any rational way because of all the preconceptions we have? When I see a drug addict on the TV I don't put it down to the drugs but the fact that the person was unable to function in the first place. Maybe that's it, it's all part of the blame culture in that we want something to blame for people fucking up, instead of accepting that people fuck up without there being anything – or anyone – else to blame. If you think about it, it is such a daft Utopian ideal to expect everyone to be perfect human beings. For some, not to be perfect is by definition the human condition.

My wife received one 'wish you were dead' letter after my trial in the Eighties, from one of the parents of a young victim of drug abuse. I really feel for the parents of the person that had died. But I really cannot accept that I am to blame for other people's actions. Am I being irresponsible? No, the child that died was messed up. The parents couldn't accept that. I am guessing here, but I think the writer of that letter wanted someone to blame instead of accepting the fact that their child was messed up. It is a feature of our modern world that people don't want to accept that we have no predetermined right to a happy and successful life. Sometimes life is fucked.

After the Jamaica debacle, things changed. I did one more trip from Amsterdam but I was finding working with Mick very difficult. He was getting really flash and I just didn't feel comfortable with him any more. I had always been able to handle him for a couple of days at time, but never for a long period, and in the months following our Caribbean trip he became totally off the wall. I didn't know what he was up to when I wasn't around, but whatever it was it seemed to be making him completely obnoxious.

I found out the reason for it all when I went over unexpectedly for a couple of days that September without telling him I was coming. He answered the door with drooping eyes, scratching his arms, and then sat nodding off in a chair once we had got up to the flat. He was on smack.

I tried to tell him but, as with alcohol, you can't make someone stop. It's tragic, but you can't do anything. You have to leave them be and wait for them to make the decision themselves – or destroy themselves. It is not that you don't care, but you get dragged in and as well as not being able to do anything to help them, you can end up being messed up yourself. So that night I said fuck it and left. I haven't seen Mick since. He's back in England now. When I ask mutual friends about him they say he's clean and I hope he is.

Something else changed my life profoundly, and beautifully, at that time. A week before that last trip to the Dam I had met the woman who I had been looking for – without knowing it – all my life. The Last Resort was still going and I would still go in quite a bit. Chris and Jackie had been to Mykonos for the summer of 1979 and came back raving about it. However, the big news for me was that they had met a beautiful woman named Mary, whom they had asked to help out in the Resort's bar. I still remember the first time I saw that woman, who is now my wife. It was love at first sight for me and even though we've been through some tough things and big fights I still feel that love. Well, as long as we are not having one of our rows…!

I returned from the Dam and my break with Mick and by October 1979 Mary and I were living together. I felt good for the first time in a long time – and it's lasted. I was so into my relationship and having broken away from the scams from the Dam I decided to start working again and try to live a normal life. I got a job running a small group of clothes shops based in Kensington and Chelsea. I continued to supply a few friends with coke, but no trips or big scams. I was happy with my girlfriend, we were having a nice time and things were running smoothly and without too much trouble. The job made me feel very safe with no paranoia, as I was just seeing a few friends. We lived just off the Kings Road and were having a great time. I was over the moon to have found the person I had been looking for all of my life.

The guy whom I had scored dope from in my first days in Carnaby Street was still a close friend and my lady and I spent a lot of time with him and his wife. He had a very successful skateboard shop in Kensington when skateboards became the in-thing and we would spend a lot of weekends at his place in Somerset. He had met a young guy called Gerry, who did bits and pieces for him. Gerry too had become a bit of a friend and we all did business together. I found it amusing that he lived in a block of flats next to Kensington police station; I would drop an ounce or two off to him and look over and into it. However, my amusement didn't last long, as he turned out to be a wrong 'un. We were never sure exactly what happened, but we believe he was busted and he gave me up as his source.

Mary and I were in bed one morning in our Flood Street flat when the door came crashing in followed by ten cops, and a Labrador, who started ripping the place apart. They weren't exactly nasty, but of course they weren't friendly either, and started hammering on about where the coke was that they knew I had. They went straight to a section of the skirting board in the hall that I had loosened and hollowed out behind to use as a stash. However there was nothing in it. It was one of those lucky days. I had one of those one-gramme coke bottles stashed in a roller blind. When the cops came in they pulled the cord and rolled it up with the bottle inside. Once they didn't find anything behind the skirting board they eased up and went for another tack. The inspector and a WPC took Mary into the kitchen where she made them a cup of tea and they sat at the kitchen table prodding and probing her while another two sat with me in the living room, trying to dig inside with queries and allusions. It was obvious from the way they angled their questions that someone knew a lot about me. Or at least as much as Gerry knew.

They finally left after an hour and we were able to sit back and relax. Well a bit. The only trouble was there were 2 kilos of coke under the kitchen floorboards that I had to get out, which were situated directly beneath where the inspector had been sitting when he was querying Mary. The dog completely missed it. Mary told me they had lifted a sisal mat that covered the floor, but as it shed all the time it looked as if it hadn't been lifted for months, so they didn't bother to lift it further. Luck is a nice thing.

The only trouble was, would they come back? Would they follow me? I had no idea. So after an hour I went for a drive around Chelsea and Fulham, checking my mirror all the time. I drove for an hour or so, stopping to go into a shop here and there, looking to see if anyone was following me. Finally I felt safe enough, went home and got the two kilos from under the floorboards. The only problem now was to get it out of the flat without looking as if I was carrying anything, so I went back to an old scamming technique, strapped them to my body and wandered out again. I felt highly exposed as I walked to the car, but once I got in and away I felt fine. I was able to drop them back to the owner later and I was clean.

That was a very close thing and it made me very nervous for a couple of months. Gerry was still working for my mate, but we couldn't let on that we thought that he had given me away, so we simply had to close up shop for a bit. After a few months he went to the States, never to be heard of again.

It's so difficult in those circumstances to ever prove that someone has put you in it. You can only surmise, you'll never know for certain. And what can you do if you do find out? Villains would say kill them or do them over. From my perspective it was always just cut them out of your life, as I am not a violent person. Anyway, what would I have gained by harming them?

After that raid, I virtually stopped scamming. Mary was rightly very nervous about us being busted again, as she had never really been involved in that sort of thing before. We moved to Fulham and I put all my energies into my job, which was going well.

However, by the spring of 1982 I was back doing some dealing when I literally bumped into a guy in the Kings Road who had been a customer at the Last Resort. We had mutual friends and over a coffee in the Picasso he told me he was bringing in large consignments of Lebanese dope and was having trouble moving it. I agreed to move some and within a week I was off-loading five drums of olive oil (again) from a truck in Glebe Place off the Kings Road. I hold my hands up once more: it was crazy the way we did those things back then.

The drums contained 100 kilos of good Lebanese in total. The only problem was getting them open. They were welded so well that it took ages to do. Still, it was a nice little scam and I worked with them for a year on that one, with 100 kilos every couple of months. Between David and myself we were able to move the dope easily through close friends.

Weirdly enough, I had no way of contacting them. I would just receive a call and a place to meet and collect my drums. I would receive another call a month later telling me where to meet and drop off the money. I never even knew the surname of the guy I met in the Kings Road. After the year I didn't receive another call until another eighteen months had passed. I went to meet the guy and it turned out that the whole scam had been busted. Some of the guys had gone down, though not the guy who was my contact. He told me that I and his other outlets were never touched as the police had never found his phone book, which he never kept at home. He had always used phone boxes, and therefore they had no way of knowing whom he had worked with. It was a bit of a shock to know that this had happened without having any idea at all at what had been going down elsewhere.

Still, I was safe. In those intervening eighteen months I had been working with David and Canadian Frank, who lived in Camden at the time with the occasional load of weed. I was working all day running the shops and a warehouse up in Hemel Hempstead and would fit drops and pick-ups into my work schedule. It was all go and everything seemed to run so easily. There never seemed to be any heat around and if my memory is right I don't remember anyone I know being busted in the years '79 to '84.

Mary and I had bought a flat in Battersea and married in February '82, which was a wonderful day. Married in Chelsea registry office and then lunch for thirty in what I still think was one of the greatest restaurants ever in London, The Bagatelle, owned by the best restauranteur ever, Danny Morocco. Goodness knows where he is now, but I wish he had another restaurant, as I find so many of them pretentious and crap these days.

There was one guest there, sadly dead now, who was to inadvertently lead me into my last big scam. Paul had been a chef for a while at the Last Resort and after leaving for the States for a couple of years had returned to work at The Embassy when it first reopened in the early Eighties. It was an insane place, with all the waiters whizzing round on roller skates. I remember tooting in the corridor leading to the kitchen with Paul while waiters came by, grabbed a line and skated on even more quickly than before.

Paul was gay. Well, I say gay, but I know several women he had affairs with. We saw a lot of him at this time and one weekend we went with him and a boyfriend to a beautiful cottage near Padstow, owned by a friend of his. The boyfriend was a Peruvian called Robbie, who was one of the most wonderful people I have ever known. During the years before his death in the late Eighties Mary and I were to become very good friends with him. He had a smile that could lighten any room and he was one of the few people I have ever known who never had a bad word to say of anyone. He was a mischievous child at heart and was always up for fun.

We all had a good time that weekend. It was one of those glorious Cornish June weekends when the sun shone and you could look down from Tintagel into the glistening Atlantic and fancy seeing Arthur's knights riding the white horses as they rolled in. Magical.

We got a bit stoned and all got on well, but I never discussed any business with Robbie. A few months later, we were at a launch party for yet another fashion magazine when we bumped into Robbie; he and I sat in a corner chatting whilst Mary cruised the room, looking beautiful and chatting to everyone, something I've never been big on. During our talk, Robbie suggested I come to Peru and meet some friends of his whom he said had the most wonderful coke. I had been wanting to go and see Peru for years but I had never met anyone who could provide the connection that Robbie was offering. I also knew that as he was such a lovely guy, there was no chance of him introducing me to any heavy gangster types.

It all took several months to come about, but eventually Robbie said he was going home for a holiday and would I go with him for a couple of weeks. It came at a very opportune time, as I had just lost my job due to being busted and I was short of money.

It had all been a very close-run thing. I had been doing the weed with David and Frank and I had taken 50 kilos – two guys I knew, who were involved with some exotic religious group who believed the world would end in 1997, wanted it. I had stashed it up at Olympia in an old bakery that a friend had access to and the guys were coming to pick it up after I had finished work.

They turned up at my flat in Battersea, sat down and then told me they were being followed. I couldn't bloody believe it. They were being followed and they just roll up at my home and tell me. I thought I'd better go out and check it out.

I went out and got into my car, drove a couple of streets to a shop and jumped a red light on the way. Sure enough, a beaten-up old Land Rover a couple of cars back accelerated through the red light and followed me. I knew they were on me and so I stopped to buy some flowers and went home. The guys were still there and I told them what had happened. I still don't know if they were just following anyone who came out of my block of flats or whether they knew who I was, but I told the guys the only good bit of news. I had been trying to get hold of the guy who had the keys to the stash all afternoon and couldn't raise him so I didn't have the dope anywhere local. I said they should just head for home, sit tight and see what happened. I told Mary what was happening when she came in and after checking the flat was clean we sat tight waiting to see what would happen.

Ten minutes after the guys left there was a knock on the door and in they came. This lot were nasty. They were a regional crime squad who obviously thought they were the Sweeney. It was ridiculous the way they postured and performed. I wasn't bothered as there was nothing in the flat and I knew they were on a loser. Then I was fucked. They found a gramme of coke that I had lost a couple of months before, under a corner of the fitted carpet in the living room. What a prat. I had completely forgotten about it. I thought I had sold it or done it myself. But no, dopey bollocks had stashed it in a stupid place when he was stoned. That was enough for them; they took Mary and I for a drive to their headquarters in Reading. Great, that was all I needed.

It turned out the other guys had been picked up as well and we were all there. The next day they let Mary go, but they charged me with possession and I was remanded to appear before magistrates in two weeks. So I was fucked. Poor Mary had the rotten job of telling my boss what had happened; although he got stoned himself, he wasn't exactly enamoured of me and my drug connections. I sat in a jail in Reading for two weeks – and no, I didn't read Oscar Wilde's Ballad of Reading Gaol. I was given a suspended sentence for the gramme and that was that. The only problem was, I was fired from my job, which was a real pain as we were really tight for money.

So that was how I came to be flying to Lima with Robbie in April 1985. I had retrieved the camera case that had accompanied me on that fruitless trip to Jamaica from my brother's loft, had taken my last $20,000 and was off doing one again.

Lima was weird. I had never met so many macho guys and as I am known for being a little sarcastic, I really had to bite my tongue sometimes. Robbie's friends were nothing like him. It was obvious that they liked him, as he was unique, but any other gays they would give more than just a hard time to. I stayed for the first few days at Robbie's mother's house, which was a beautiful Spanish colonial mansion in Miraflores. I enjoyed the company of his eccentric mother, who was a Spanish grand dame living as if she was in Madrid rather than Lima – jarringly incongruous when you saw the poverty that was everywhere in the city. While I was staying there, Robbie took me out to lunch and dinner with his old university friends, who were the ruling elite of Peru. They were all of Spanish descent and I didn't meet any metitzos at all. It was a Europe of thirty years before transported and time-warped – all very nice, but I could not feel comfortable in this world preserved in aspic. Everyone took coke in the clubs we went to and it was incredible stuff – a pinkish flake that we rarely saw in London.

The third day I was there things changed. Robbie took me out to the beach at Porto Agrmosa and a magnificent house looking out over the Pacific and, some thousands of miles beyond the horizon, Japan. I was introduced to a small, stocky Peruvian Indian who was to have a profound effect on my life in the next five years. His name was Coci, pronounced 'cocky', and he sure was. He didn't stop from the minute I met him until the last time I saw him. Coci was a chemist who had the hardest job in the production of coke. The process requires a really good chemist to be involved and Coci, so he told me, was one of the best. He assured me that his services were always in demand by producers. Coci also was sending coke on a regular basis to the States; he wasn't really interested in Europe as he felt it was far too complicated compared to sending to the States. However, he said he was prepared to give me whatever I wanted as a favour to Robbie at a price of $5,000 a kilo. This was excellent news for me, as that meant I could make approximately £20,000 on each kilo I took back. As I wanted 4 kilos, that would be £80,000, which seemed pretty good to me. The only thing was that he wanted me to stay at the beach house until I was to return to London, as he was very security conscious.

After a couple of days of sybaritic lounging in the sun I was surprised by Coci's return. Much to my pleasure, he announced: 'We go to jungle tomorrow.' I felt like bloody Tarzan, but I knew what he meant. I had obviously got across to him how much I wanted to see how and where the coke was produced and I was off on a jaunt. Great!

If you ever want to lose weight in a hurry, just go to the Amazonian jungle of Peru for a few days. I have experienced humidity at various locations around the world, but the intensity of it on that trip to the jungle was unbelievable. My eyes were sore within minutes from the amount of salt water that dribbled into them. Mind you, it gave me the opportunity to adopt a very natty line in bandanas. And I wouldn't have missed that trip for anything.

The whole production was, and is, carried on high in the Andes and deep in the jungle. It's almost a terrorist activity. The distribution is totally isolated from the production. This is obviously deliberately done by those controlling the industry to keep all the profits in their pockets. I was very lucky to meet the farmers on that trip, as other people who have scammed coke I have spoken to have never met anyone but the middlemen in the cities, which is a shame, as it takes an awful lot of the experience away and does undeniably make it into just a business.

After that trip I was to realise that the world approach – and particularly the approach of the Americans – towards cocaine control is absolute rubbish. All the gangsters, cartels and the like could be wiped out cheaply and efficiently. The farmers who grow the coca do so because it is the best cash crop going. All the Americans and the rest of the West have to do is pay them more than they get for the cocoa to produce another crop. Of course, they would have to pay them well, as the estimated profit on a kilo of coke is estimated to be approximately 20,000 per cent. They are only getting a few cents per kilo and compared to the cost of armies, drug agents, boats, planes and surveillance equipment used further down the line, it would be nothing.

Of course, this is where the fact that drug enforcement is a major industry comes into play. Just think. If all those farmers weren't producing coke, what would all those companies that produce the equipment used in the drugs war do for income? What would all the police and other government employees do for a job? Of course, the biggest thing is the banks' income from all of this. I am in no way a conspiracy theorist, but it seems obvious to me that there are an awful lot of people who have a very serious vested interest in the continuation of the drugs war.

The same thing would apply if governments were to legalise drugs. Where would those companies make profits then, and what would all those redundant cops do for a job? I suppose the cops could open drug boutiques with their redundancy pay. Now there's an awful thought: scoring from an ex-cop. Ughh! Don't think it will happen, do you?

Even the use of that phrase 'drugs war' is a perfect example of the use of language to evoke the right sub-conscious response in the public. 'Stamping on Peruvian peasants' doesn't have the same ring, does it? Governments go on about fighting the drugs war, but they make no effort to stop the movement of the large sums of money involved. If they really wanted to, they could very easily stop the global transference of these monies. However, banks and financial institutions don't want the estimated $600 billion cash cow of drugs profits to be taken out of the system.

After that trip into the mountains I returned to Coci's beachhouse for the last week. The house had servants and a pool and was set in two-thirds of an acre of gardens, so I managed to cope. I was able to relax, get a tan and read all of the books I had brought with me. Tough life, huh?

However there was definitely no chance of popping out to the shops, as the whole house was within a compound and there was an armed guard at the gate. I didn't see Coci again until two days before I was due to leave; he had stayed in the Amazon in his capacity as chemist.

When he came back he brought my 4 kilos and it was beautiful coke. Probably the best I have ever had. It was what is called Peruvian flake; it looked and shimmered like slivers of mother of pearl and gave you a really gentle buzz. The thing about that quality of coke is that it requires a skilled chemist to bring it out that way and it requires good chemicals, such as pure alcohol, in the finishing process, which they can no longer do, or can't be bothered to do. The market is so great now that I presume the producers work on an industrial scale rather than a craft one. I have alluded earlier to dope being produced as a fine wine would be and that is the best analogy for coke production as well.

I say that all the coke was like that, but that's not strictly speaking true, as I was only going by a small bag of about 10 grammes Coci had brought loose. The 4 kilos had been pressed into four small blocks, each about half the size of a 2-lb bag of sugar and vacuum-packed; therefore, I didn't want to open them, as they were packed ready to go. In retrospect, I suppose it seems odd the way I simply trusted him, as he could just as easily have been given me four bags of flour for my $20,000. Mad? I don't know. I just trusted the guy after being given the run of his house for a week. And his house certainly didn't suggest he was desperate for that sort of money.

Robbie came out with a half a dozen friends the night Coci returned and we were up all night drinking Pisco Sours, tooting and, just as in London, solving the problems of the world in a stoned, non-stop conversation. I felt very at home.

Coci and I spent my last night discussing the possibilities of finding a way to ship coke to Europe. However, the problems were that he was quite happy with his business to the States and I had no realistic means of transport other than body packing, which wouldn't have worked on a large enough scale for him. By the end of the night we had only vague ideas, but we agreed to keep in touch and he told me I was welcome to return whenever I wanted to do body scams.

A few hours later I was being driven to the airport in Coci's chauffeur-driven Merc. I felt really comfortable. It was nice not to be strapped up with stuff, as it was really humid, and I was very pleased with the false bottom camera case. The only problem was the weight. It did feel heavy, so I didn't want anybody handling it. I knew that it would be alright in any X-ray machine. It was just that if customs wanted it opened I would have to make sure I did the opening. Lima airport was pretty chaotic, with lots of military and cops, and I did see a couple of dogs, but it wasn't organised in a systematic way. They only seemed to be checking Peruvians and I cruised straight though.

All I had to worry about now was Madrid, as once I was through there I would be on an internal European flight to London and my plan was to walk straight out of there with just the camera case and go back for my suitcase the following day. We stopped over in Caracas and then it was Madrid here we come. I breezed through there too; I can't even remember it, it was so smooth. Well, almost.

I remember sitting in the transit lounge waiting to board when two cops came in and walked around, obviously looking for someone. Beirut jumped back to my mind, firing all of the fight-or-flight neurones in my brain. Luckily, before I ran for the door they went to a guy sitting opposite me. However, those few seconds, when they were walking up and past me, definitely made me a possible coronary patient. It was over in seconds, but it took a while for me to get my adrenaline levels down and feel relax and composed again. The flights worked out perfectly and I arrived at Heathrow at 9 p.m., when customs tend to be winding their numbers down, and I walked through without seeing one of them. Yessssss!

Now came the hard bit. I hadn't told Mary where I was going when I left. Well, I had sort of. I'd said I was going to Spain to see David about maybe doing something with him. She knew he had no phone where he lived and I'd told her when I'd be back. I hadn't told her the whole story, as I didn't want her worrying. Now it had come off I was desperate to get home and celebrate with her.

I charged into the flat about 10.30 p.m. full of it and woke Mary up. Big mistake. I spent the next five minutes getting it in the neck for having a suntan and a good time while she had been working every day, and not even bothering to ring. The trouble was, I wasn't listening I just thought let Mary get that out of her system and then tell her.

Well, when she paused for breath I did. Another big mistake. Everything from an Art-Deco lamp to her glasses came flying at me, along with shouts of: 'You bastard! You did that without telling me. Get out! Get out!'

I knew when she was serious, and so the big scammer took his camera case, got his car keys from the kitchen, went downstairs and off to a hotel room for the night feeling very deflated.

Oddly enough, looking back at when I was scamming, my only real problems were nothing to do with business but in trying to keep things right at home. We made up the next day but it wasn't without a certain amount of nastiness on both sides. I really did understand how Mary felt. It was always a problem when I was doing something of how to deal with it at home. Some guys I knew didn't care and others would share the decisions with their wives or girlfriends. With Mary it was always difficult because, as she said many times, it wasn't the fact that I was doing it that upset her, but that it might cause us to be separated. The upside can be so great that you always want to go ahead with another scam; the downside is so potentially catastrophic that it is unthinkable. So you tend not to think about it.

Really, the only answer is to be single, but that requires being a different sort of guy to me. I sit here now thinking about it and can honestly say there is no answer to this problem if you are in a loving relationship and also involved in scamming.

CHAPTER TWELVE

A BUST AND A
NEW SCAM

AFTER THE TRIP to Lima I immediately sold 1 kilo wholesale for £25,000. Thereby I had my initial investment back and another five grand. As I've said before, I didn't like working with people I didn't know, so I sold the other 3 kilos off for £1,000 an ounce, which would have totalled £105,000 if I hadn't given any away or done any myself. Still, even after allowing for personal use and gifts I did pretty well. It took six months to clear but I was in no rush.

During that six months I was keeping an eye open for a business to put some money into, as I didn't like doing nothing. I know it sounds perverse, but I didn't get off on the same old round of going out to lunch and hanging out with friends; it had lost its charm and I found it repetitious and boring. Some of my friends were, and still are, quite comfortable with that way of life, but I suppose there is some trace of Puritan guilt in me about being idle. Mind you, I could still lunch with the best of them if I was in the mood. So don't think I'd become a killjoy.

The upshot of this search for a business was to have far-reaching consequences at a later date. But I'm getting ahead of myself. Before returning to teaching, Mary had been running a very trendy shop in the Kings Road owned by an old friend in the fashion world and had worked with a beautiful Swedish girl whom I had known since the Sixties. We had never been that close but when she started working with Mary we started seeing a lot of her and her boyfriend Pat, a nice guy, who was also someone I had come across through friends. He and I got talking one late night and he suggested we start a security company specialising in fancy grills for expensive houses. He had a few contacts in the business and it didn't require a large initial investment, so without much thought I put the money up and we started the company.

Pat is a really nice Irish guy in the Bob Geldof mould – mind you he'll hate me for making the comparison. He was really keen to get the business working and was very busy from day one. The trouble was, I didn't know anything about the business and couldn't contribute that much. I would go into the office in Clapham every day and sit there and do nothing. OK, it got me out of the house, but I was going crazy within a couple of months.

I was still clearing the 3 kilos and my people would pop into the office to collect whatever they needed and drop any cash they had for me. There is no doubt about it. When you have cash you spend it, and the trouble is, you don't think about it while you're doing it. Well, I didn't. Mary and I spent an awful lot of money at this time. We were always going away for weekends and eating out. I think we would eat in maybe once a week and we definitely spent a lot on clothes. I never saw our lifestyle as ostentatious, although I'm probably being rather defensive in hindsight. I also acquired an interest in antique watches at that time and started going to the markets and auctions on a regular basis.

One of those trips to an auction and too much casualness was to lead to near disaster one day. I was going to an auction at Sotheby's and my friend from the Carnaby Street days wanted to come along as it was his wife's birthday in a couple of days and he was looking for a watch.

We agreed to meet in Kensington High Street, as he was going from his shop and I didn't want to take my car. At this time he was working a scam that involved kilos of coke that he was clearing. I knew what he was doing but wasn't involved.

It was one of those lovely cold but bright autumn days and we were both in excellent spirits and looking forward to the day ahead. When I got in the car he said to me, 'You don't mind if we just pop up to Notting Hill do you? I've got to drop off a kilo to Tom.' Of course, I said I didn't mind at all. Writing it now, I can't believe how blasé I was but that's what happens when you are involved with it all. Being around when deals are being done just sort of happened. Crazy.

We went to go up Camden Hill Road, when suddenly a beaten-up old Lancia pulled across in front of us from the opposite lane and two guys jumped out.

'Cops!' Bobby shouted.

The next thing I know, he'd put his foot down, smashed the Lancia out of the way and surged up Camden Hill Road with something hanging off the front and making a din as it scraped along the road. As we got to the top of the hill by the Windsor Castle, he screamed right down a one-way street.

'The kilo's in the glove box,' he shouted to me.

I grabbed it and looked to throw it out, but I looked behind and there was a cop car just turning into the road. 'They're on us,' I shouted back.

He accelerated and shot out into Kensington Church Street and then took a hard turning left into a side road. In front of us was a dustcart parked at the side of the road, and as we passed it I threw the kilo in the back. Luckily I had gloves on as it was a cold day, so if it was found it wouldn't have my dabs on it.

Bobby was now heading up another one-way street the wrong way towards Notting Hill. 'I'm out of here,' I said, as he slowed at the Bayswater Road. I jumped out and slammed the door whilst he was trying to get out on the busy road, just making it as he surged off. I looked around. No one had really taken any notice. I looked back down to where we had come from and a cop car with siren blaring turned a corner and headed straight for me. I turned and walked, although desperate to run, to the tube, down the steps and onto the platform, where I sat watching the stairs. After a minute or two I was sure I hadn't been seen getting out of the car.

I went to Earls Court and tried to phone Bobby's wife but the phone was answered by a voice I didn't recognise, which said, 'Who's that?'

I knew that it was cops. They had obviously busted his house.

I wasn't that bothered, as I wasn't involved, so I headed home and made sure our place was clear. I put the clothes, shoes and gloves I'd been wearing into a bag and got rid of them. The only reason they might know me was if I had been spotted during some previous observations.

The next morning, Bobby's wife phoned me and asked me to pop round to their house. He had finally been stopped after writing off six cop cars and they weren't very happy. The big bummer came when she said that some dustman had found the kilo of coke in their cart and handed it into the cops. It later transpired that his dabs were on it and it helped to convict him and four others. My name never came up and if they did know about me they knew I wasn't involved, so they left me out of it. Which was nice.

After that I was very careful for a while, but there is no doubt that unless you have iron discipline the longer things go well the more you feel safe. Which, of course, you're not. You don't check your mirror as often as you should, you don't watch what you say on the phone and you can't be bothered to go out to the phone box when it's raining. All those little things start happening and you can get into trouble.

However, I wasn't thinking about such things right then. I was more concerned about the way the security company was going. It was about nine months after my return from Peru and through no one's fault the company just wasn't working. I had about £60,000 in cash but I had no income and I knew that due to the way we lived this could disappear very quickly.

We just didn't seem to be able to get much work. And there was one job we nearly got that, in retrospect, I'm really glad we didn't. What happened was, the guy who had done the Lebanese in the oil drums resurfaced and he would occasionally score some coke from me. However, we didn't do any serious business and would just meet for lunch every now and then and have a chat. At one of these lunches, I told him about the problems with the security business and he said in passing that he thought he knew someone who might give us some work. I didn't think any more about it until he rang me a couple of weeks later.

He said that there was a mate of his who lived in Kent and needed his security system upgraded. I went down and found myself in a paranoid's dream: the place was wired up and fenced all around. The thing I remember most of all were the two copies of fake Elizabethan mansions that were the kennels for two Rottweilers. The guy was desperate to get a nightsight surveillance system installed, something that was way beyond our capabilities, and I told him that we couldn't help and left.

It was only later when I saw the house on the news and heard that a policeman had been killed there that the name rang bells. Kenny Noye. I knew nothing about him and was just glad that I hadn't been involved with the security. I had sussed when I'd gone there that he fancied himself a bit but I never knew who he was or anything about him as I never had any dealings with villains.

Besides that possible job and a few others, our security company really wasn't doing anything. I had thought about trying to put something together again from Peru. The problem was, I had had no contact with Coci since leaving Peru. Although Robbie had been home a couple of times, he had not been able to get in touch with him. Anyway, I wasn't really in a rush to go back and do another camera case run, as I hadn't really enjoyed the trip.

Besides, things were getting very noisy in the press and on TV with regard to coke, with that crap band 'Maggie and the Fascists' full of blood and thunder. So I was concentrating on trying to find a business to put my money into.

Then, out of the blue, in March 1985 I had a call from Coci to tell me he was in London and asking me to meet him at a friend's flat in Putney. This really was unexpected, as he hadn't even mentioned that he knew anyone in London and from what he'd said in Peru he wasn't really interested in Europe. I was even more surprised when I went over to Putney and he was staying with two gay guys – one real Peruvian queen and his boyfriend, an English immigration officer of all things.

It was good to see Coci, as he's a nice guy, if rather macho and noisy. He spent the first half an hour going on about a motorbike he'd bought to send back home. Crazy, he comes all that way and here he was going on like a kid with a new toy. Anyway, after he'd finished raving about the bike he got down to business. The upshot was that he knew an American couple in their sixties who wanted to bring a couple of kilos at a time into England. They were art dealers who dealt in Peruvian art and came to London twice a year to see antiquities dealers. The method was simple: they would be bringing fabric hangings that would be mounted on wood plaques and Coci was going to have the coke pressed into the right shape and inserted into the plaques; then a sheet of a veneer would be applied and the hangings would be mounted on them.

The nice thing was that the wood would not be totally obscured by the hanging and therefore, psychologically, it would not appear to be hidden by the fabric. It's useful if you are smuggling something to have it almost in the open, as the customs are not immediately thinking 'What's under there?' It sounds daft, but it really does work. I said I was perfectly happy to clear the coke but that I didn't want to meet the Americans. Coci told me that was no problem as he would be coming to Europe to coincide with their trips. So that was that.

A couple of months later, Coci called me over to Putney and handed me the first of these mounting boards. I never got to see the fabrics, which was a shame. It was a pain getting the veneer off of the coke though, as they had glued it onto the plastic in which it was wrapped, and when I went to ease it off the plastic it ripped and I ended up with 2 kilos of coke all over the floor. Very, very irritating. I don't know if you know this, but if you drop coke on the floor and try to collect it up you collect every grain of dust and fluff as well. Which means you end up with a dirty grey mess that no one wants. So I spent the next 4 hours sifting the coke to remove all the muck. Now that was bad enough, but on top of that I was also touching the coke, and before I knew it I was off my face. It was a nightmare: to be stoned and hyper trying sort all this gunk out was no fun. When I had finally done, I found I was an ounce short. Anyway, I cleared the 2 kilos for £50,000 each and gave Coci £30,000. A nice little touch, and very handy.

CHAPTER THIRTEEN

CATERING AND COKE SMUGGLING

MARY AND I met Eddie Cowell in 1986 when he was going out with an old friend of hers. He and his partner owned a wine bar in London.

Eddie is one of life's charmers, small, energetic, ever-ready with a smile and a one-liner and enough syrup to drown a pancake. He's of a slighter older generation than me and he missed out on the drugs of the Sixties, as he had been in the merchant navy at the time. However, I have to admit I always really enjoyed his company and sense of fun. Although we didn't really have a lot in common, we would see one another every few weeks and go out for lunch or dinner. On one such occasion he came up with a business idea that I was really sold on. What a mug.

Eddie had become involved in the trendy world of advertising since being in London and had fancied setting up a mobile catering company to provide location catering. He told me that he knew a couple who were getting out of the business and wanted to sell their fitted-out catering truck cheaply; Eddie assured me he had enough connections to get work almost immediately. He said all we would need on top of the truck was a base in London to do all the prep. He had two people to work with us and it would require £20,000 to get started. I agreed to provide the cash readily enough, as the security company was a dead loss and I had to find something to do with my money and time.

We got going and the work soon proved to be fun, even if we had to work very long hours. I knew a few people doing videos and with Eddie's contacts as well we got known quickly and were doing alright, although we were hardly making a fortune. Still, I wasn't overly bothered as I had just done the first one of the fabric scams and I knew another was due in a few months. I was cash rich and was now involved in a business that seemed to have potential. Things were looking good.

I really enjoyed working on location. We would leave the yard at any time between three and seven in the morning and head off to whatever English idyll of a village was being used to sell cornflakes or soap powder. You would rarely be called on to set up in the dingy suburbs. It was always the Home Counties or the extremities of Cornwall, Wales or Scotland. No reality here please, we're selling nirvana.

I had spent all of my adult life working within a small group of people, whether I was scamming or doing normal jobs, and I was expecting the advertising world to be different. However it didn't differ that much: everybody knew one another and you would see the same people from week to week. There was also a healthy drug culture within the business. Everyone earnt such phenomenal amounts of money that it really was a case of spend, spend, spend. I got a nice little business going with one of the guys working for us, whereby he would sell grammes of coke while serving lunch. I didn't make a lot, but it gained us quite a bit of work for the company in the long run: if we were on the job, the production companies knew they could get some toot.

The only trouble with this world was the pretentiousness of some of the people. You would think they were creating

Battleship Potemkin instead of a chocolate bar ad the way some of them went on. The videos were more fun and the creativity seemed far greater; what's more, they tended to be much more anarchic, drug-fuelled projects. It's interesting to note that there wasn't any less efficiency on these shoots compared to the pretentious ones.

Eddie was in his element on a shoot, always cracking jokes. The only problem was that he was not keen on actually doing any work. Still, his function was to be the face of the company and he was good at it.

The other two members of the team were Fatboy and Julie. Fatboy was really E's batman and factotum. He was a roly-poly cook, not the brightest cookie on the block but a jovial presence. Julie was the Delia Smith of our operation and, although not up to Delia's standard, was undoubtedly good at her job. Unfortunately, Eddie treated her terribly. I never knew if they'd had a thing in the past but there was a tension there that I was always having to diffuse. Still, we had a good time on the whole.

That year seemed to fly by, what with the work and Coci's Americans making three trips. Mary and I flew off for long weekends in Paris, Florence, wherever, and for a month in Greece during the summer. I spent a lot of money having our flat in Battersea renovated by an interior designer friend. It looked beautiful when it was finished and was such a comfortable flat that every weekend it would be full of friends until God knows what hour. It was a great year and one during which I acquired a taste for Cristal champagne. Naff, I know, but it's true.

You may wonder how you combine selling drugs and holding down a job or running a business. The truthful answer is, it's not difficult. The hard part is getting the motivation to get up and go to work for eight, ten or twelve hours a day when you know you only need to do three hours of work a week to make a few grand.

The actual running of the two businesses is not a problem when you have your sources and distribution worked out as I did. I would see my guys once or twice a week at prearranged meeting places and we would swap drugs and money. That was it, done; it would only take up an hour or so at most, so time was no problem. Occasionally I would have to take a day off to sort out a shipment or something similar, but that was the same as anyone in a legit profession taking a day off sick.

The problems came when I would have to get up at four o'clock after being out until two o'clock and it was freezing cold and I knew I had a twelve-hour day in front of me in some muddy field with some pretentious PA talking to me like a piece of shit, all the while knowing that I didn't really have any need to get up. Of course, the truth was I did need to get up: I was able to feel comfortable with my scamming and dealing due to the fact that I was always working.

You see, the thing with the cops or the customs is, if they don't have any firm info on you, but maybe have some vague intelligence that you might be at it, they don't just come round and bust you. They flop on you once a week, or once a month, and probably monitor your phone. As one of them said to me at a later date, 'We've got a lot more time than you. We can wait, go away and come back later.' Now this is true, but if you are in regular employment they are going to be far more likely to leave you alone and go raid a guy who doesn't leave his house all day but has people calling round all the time and then goes out until four in the morning. Because they just aren't sure if you are at it.

The phone monitoring is the big one, though. If you talk business on the phone, they are going to have you. Do you know that they have programmes that check for key phrases such as 'tickets' and 'T-shirts', which are often used as pseudonyms for cocaine? If you use such phrases the system flags you for closer inspection. Another thing about the phone monitoring is that the Home Office claims that all phone monitoring has to be signed off by the Home Secretary. This is an out and out lie. The reason they never admit to phone tapping is that they can't use it in court, so they have absolutely no need to admit the use of such clandestine monitoring.

One time I was being questioned and they asked me who a certain person was. Well the thing was, I hadn't this person's address or phone number and I hadn't mentioned him to anyone. He had simply rung me one day out of the blue to make contact after ten years. By the way, he lived in the States and never rang again or came to England prior to my being questioned. So how the hell else could they have known he existed other than having a phone tap on me? I don't care really – all's fair in love and war – but it is illegal …

Another thing with me was that I got bored not doing

anything and just would rather be out working than sitting around. And you must remember that Mary would be going to her school every day to teach, so it wasn't as if we were able to just hang out all the time. I suppose we could have, but we weren't, and aren't, those kind of people.

The only other problem was healthy paranoia. Healthy paranoia differs from the normal kind in that when you do what I did, you really do have to develop a set of habits that are vital to your survival. You have to be careful when you meet people, not so much in a working environment but when you are in a social situation such as a bar, a club or maybe a party. You have to watch who is there and what they are up to and mind your conversation. Nothing too paranoid, but you have to be aware of the possibility that the person you are talking to could just as easily not be what they seem. I always found this difficult, particularly if I was at a friend's party, for example, and got talking to someone I liked. I didn't want to have feed them a load of bullshit; I wasn't hung up about what my second profession was, but I couldn't be honest with them until I'd known them for a long time on the whole.

Of course, sometimes I met someone whom a close friend said was cool, and that was alright, although I'd still be wary. Also, I was lucky in that I was not desperate to be friends with people. I had my very close friends already and was not out to impress or be buddies with new faces. I always found it hysterical at trendy dos and dinner parties that people would suck up to stars or anyone vaguely well known. When I was catering on location, I always kept in the background. I had no need to impress or look to make friends. I left all that to Eddie, who is a champion arse licker.

My healthy paranoia did cause some friction between Mary and I, though. She is one of the world's great talkers and socialisers and many a night she would be chatting with someone in a club or some social gathering and suddenly it would be, 'Let's go to their place or back to ours', and I would try and stop it happening. Of course, she always managed to talk me into it.

Although I may refer to life being easy while I was doing scams and dealing, in all honesty there was always an underlying problem that would never go away: the effect it had on my marriage. Mary had never been involved with anyone like me before we met. I have never really asked her, but I suppose there was an element of excitement for her in being a part of this shadowy side of life, if only tangentially.

As I say, that year was rolling along quietly enough. Then I got a call from Coci asking me to go to Berlin and pick up 3 kilos from his brother, who was stuck there knowing no one. I just couldn't say no. It would be fun and I would take my old mate David, as he was really short of money at the time and would be glad of £6,000 for carrying it back. I rang him, we met and after I told him what we would be doing I gave him the money to buy a ticket for the first flight to Berlin the following day.

* * *

It was one of those dark, wet and windy October mornings when you think how far away summer seems and groan.

We had arranged to rendezvous at Heathrow at 8 a.m. as the flight to Berlin left at 9 a.m. I was sitting in the coffee shop with £45,000 in hundred-dollar bills in my pocket, waiting for my old mate David to arrive. It was getting late and his lateness certainly wasn't helping my paranoia.

When you are doing a scam, every sense is heightened, every person you look at is a potential undercover policeman. I went into Smiths, bought a paper and strolled to the coffee shop and a guy who was in the shop followed me in. Now this was a totally normal occurrence, a non-event if you like, but I spent the next ten minutes, until he left for his flight, thinking he was one of them and watching his every move from the corner of my eye. Of course, if the customs had really been watching me they wouldn't have needed to do this, as they have a very large array of cameras and viewing spots throughout the airport. However, your mind is so busy at picking up any little clue or nuance of being observed in such situations that at times logic gets lost. Especially as you are striving to behave normally. It sounds absurd to talk of trying to be normal, but when you are in the middle of a bit of business, being normal requires a superhuman effort.

Then David arrived. There was I, dressed in an Armani suit and raincoat carrying a leather attaché case, looking like all the other men off to Berlin on a day's business, and in he walks looking like a Martian, or as good as. My first thought was, 'I want to go home.'

Yes, he was wearing a suit, but it was a beige linen summer suit, more suited to the South of France in June than Berlin in October. However, it wasn't just the suit that was a problem. To start with, there were the bloody shoes, tan ostrich-skin loafers. These shoes were one of his prize possessions but they were horrendous, they had these huge nobbles on them where the feathers had been pulled and they certainly were not subtle. I always thought of them as pimp shoes. David himself looked as if he had been up all night, which was a near-certainty, and as he was 6 foot 4 inches with a broken nose, he was not anonymous. All in all, he was definitely not helping my paranoia. Of course, I couldn't talk to him as we were not supposed to be together. What good would it do it if I could? It wasn't as if he could go home and change. Anyway, knowing him he would have come back wearing something more outrageous just for the heck of it. And he certainly couldn't have got rid of the grey pallor without going to bed for a couple of days.

Of course, I wasn't really surprised, as this was David's modus operandi, but he always gave you the willies. He was a one-off who really didn't give a shit, as he believed he was untouchable. He achieved his success as a scammer by behaving so crazily that no one would possibly believe that he was doing anything illegal. I had seen him in Morocco in '68, at Tangier airport, start to remove his clothes and rant in his best English public schoolboy French as a customs officer was about to open a rug that contained 10 kilos of hash. The officer obviously thought to himself, Do I really want to see this crazy Englishman naked? So he quickly gesticulated David through. David, never being one to let things go once he had started, made his way over to a heavily braided senior officer who was wearing dark glasses, and continued his rant. Now this paragon of Moroccan justice was a man you or I would have avoided like the plague, as he exuded the air of a Tonton Macoute. I remember praying to myself, 'Leave it David! Please God, leave it now!' Still, he continued until the officer burst into laughter, ordered a junior to pick up the rug and, taking David by the arm, personally escorted him to the waiting plane. Amazing.

Thankfully, before I could get any more paranoid – especially about his hand-painted silk tie – they made the final call for the Berlin flight. David and I sat way apart on the flight and I settled into the Telegraph crossword in peace and anonymity. Of course David, as you can imagine, was anything but quiet, chatting up the stewardesses in a voice that increased in volume as he downed a continuous stream of brandies and coffee. Thank goodness it was only an hour-and-a-half flight.

Tempelhof was a bit unnerving, as the place was crawling with sub-machine-gun-wielding police in black coveralls, due to recent terrorist activity in Germany. I was out of the airport in fifteen minutes and in a cab to the hotel, where I was to meet Jorge, Coci's brother, with 3 kilos of flake to sell. I didn't know Jorge, but as I knew Coci I figured it would go easily. Coci asked me to go as they didn't know anyone in Berlin other than a guy he had been sent to see who had been busted while he was on his way to Berlin. The plan was that I would make my way to the hotel bar, meet Jorge, go to his room and do the business.

Then I would collect David from a bar down the street, return and strap him up with the 3 kilos, then catch the 6 o'clock flight back to London. Well, that was the plan.

Berlin was as grey and wet as London and I spent the twenty-minute ride to the hotel casually glancing behind to check the cab wasn't being followed. I arrived at the small, drab hotel fifteen minutes early for the 12.30 meeting. The hotel was a nightmare. I had expected to be in a large, bustling Hilton-type of establishment. Instead, it was just a doorway in one of those monotonous, grey, granite streets that run on and on in the suburbs of Berlin. It smelt of boiled cabbage and was more of a hostel with a small reception desk with a box-like office behind and rooms on two or three floors above. The sort of place where you would not be surprised to see Michael Caine as Harry Palmer struggling with some Stasi goon. I walked past the empty reception to the bar where we were to meet, which was more of a booth at the side of the lobby than any bar I knew. I ordered a beer from a very morose barman who obviously hadn't served a drink for the last month and sat at one of the three small, dust-covered tables that faced the lobby, waiting for Jorge to appear. I found myself becoming more and more uncomfortable as the clock edged around to 12.45, with still no sign of Jorge. Coci had only given me the vaguest description of his brother: 'He looks like all of us. Small, dark and swarthy. Anyway, he will be there and I've told him what you look like so he'll introduce himself and you'll be in his room doing the business within five minutes.'

However, it was now approaching one o'clock and I couldn't sit at the empty bar of this dump much longer without the barman, who sat grunting as he read his newspaper, becoming suspicious. Moreover, I knew David would be getting laid into the bar down the street and I could definitely live without that.

Not only was I aware of becoming conspicuous, my super-aware brain was also starting to edge towards the possibilities of a set-up or a rip-off. Why hadn't I ever asked Coci for his surname? At least then I could have asked at the desk if he was a resident. The £45,000 in my pocket was beginning to feel as if it was blinking through my suit. While I was busy feeding my paranoias with a panoply of such disastrous scenarios, I was startled from my reverie by a female German voice, which asked in accented English:

'Are you Herr Carter?'

What should I say? Was she a cop? As I fumbled in my brain for a response she continued:

'Herr Garcia is on the phone for you.'

The alarm bells stopped ringing. Her tone was that of someone simply doing their job. It had to be Jorge with a surname like that.

'Thank you. Where is the phone?'

With a nod, she indicated a hooded perspex booth next to the front door. As I walked the few yards to the phone, my mind began racing again while I tried to presume what he would say and what was going on. I picked up the phone.

'Hello.'

'Hello. Is that Mister Carter?'

'Yes.'

'This is Jorge. I am sorry I am not there. I move this morning.'

Jesus! What was this guy up to? I've got David down the road getting pissed. We've got a flight to catch in three hours. I really didn't need this.

'Hello. Mr. Carter are you there?'

'Yes. Where are you?'

'I am in apartment ten minutes from you.'

My mind was racing now. Was it a set-up? OK calm down, see what he says. 'Yes. So what am I to do? I was supposed to meet you here.'

'I know, but I got this place as I thought it was better for us.'

It was one of those situations where you just have to go with your feelings. I knew Coci pretty well and I was here now. Fuck it. Just go for it.

'OK. Give me the address. I'll be with you as soon as I can and I'll have my friend with me.'

He gave me the address and I walked quickly from the hotel out onto the street, which seemed even greyer than before.

I could see the sign of the bar where David was, hopefully, waiting and not pissed. Thankfully, the bar was crowded and busy serving lunch. David was ensconced in a corner booth, munching his way through a plate of sausage and sauerkraut and a stein of beer. I sank down at the table opposite him, grateful to see a friendly face in what was becoming a very alien town. I gave him an update of the situation and, thankfully, he agreed with my decision to carry on. He finished his lunch and we went out and hailed a cab, giving the address I had been given, without having the foggiest idea of where we were going and what we were walking into.

Time was now pressing. It was 2.15 and we only had about three hours to get back to the airport for our flight. The two of us were now flying on adrenaline, giving up all pretence of taking care. Ten minutes later we were ringing the intercom on yet another grey, granite building somewhere in those uniform suburbs of Berlin. We both were scanning up and down the street. Pointlessly, of course, as if things were on top now there was bugger all we could do about it.

I recognised Jorge's voice over the intercom and he buzzed us in, telling us to make for the fourth floor. We came out of the lift to a dimly lit and dirty hall to be met by a young guy of twenty-one or so; he was stoned and twitchy. The funny thing was, it made me relax. I had spent the last few hours being supersensitive and edgy about being normal and together, and now I was confronted by a stoned mule. It was all so obvious: here was this kid in on his first run, frightened and a long way from home. As he turned to lead us into the flat, David and I exchanged a look and a half-smile.

Jorge lead us into a grubby bedsit that could have been transported to Earls Court and not have been out of place. Except for the smell of sauerkraut. He indicated for us to sit on a mangy sofa and as he sat himself down, I saw the gun for the first time. I don't know anything about guns, and don't want to. This thing was small, but Jorge's sweaty hand went to it, pulled it from his waistband and just loosely held it while he used his other hand to wipe the sweat from his brow. He'd obviously seen too many crap gangster movies and I really didn't need this. I knew that he was running on coke and far twitchier that we had ever been that day. I just had to stay cool and get him to calm down and trust us. I could see it wasn't that he was out to rip us, it was that he was terrified that we were there to rip him. Oh, the joys of drug dealing!

Jorge sat wiping his brow and chewing, all the while holding the gun limply in his hand. I had to get him to calm down, as he was so wired up. I told him I'd spoken to Coci last night and that he had told me how cool Jorge was and as I was talking I took the money from my inside pocket and laid it on the table in front of me. I could see this was having the desired effect, as Jorge placed the gun on the table and settled back into the armchair. He then started to talk quickly; his heavy South American accent made his sentences very difficult to follow. It seems he had been in Berlin a week and we were the first people he had seen whom he had any knowledge of. He had arrived and phoned Colombia to ask where to go and had been told to sit tight and await instructions. Since then, he had been ringing home every day and was down to his last two hundred dollars and was terrified he'd have to return carrying the goods. The poor bastard had obviously been at the parcel, which was the worst thing he could have done. Being alone holding 3 kilos of coke in an unknown city and getting stoned was definitely not the way to handle the situation. He rabbited on for a few more minutes and finally ground to a stop. He was obviously thinking of having another line now and it gave me the opportunity to ask if we could see the goods.

He got up from the chair, glanced at the gun, decided he didn't need it and made his way to the sink behind him. He bent and opened the cupboard under the sink and then rose and turned holding a carrier bag, which he dropped on the table in front of me. I opened the bag and there were the 3 kilos in six heavily pressed and wrapped packages. I say six, but there were actually five sealed packages and one open one – which was obviously the one that he had been dipping into. This was a bloody nuisance. I didn't know how much exactly he had helped himself to; this stuff worked out at £15 per gramme wholesale and a lot more retail but I had no scales to check how much was missing. Still, it didn't look as if he'd had more than a few grammes and considering the state he was in it would be easier (and safer) to work out any discrepancies with Coci when I next saw him.

I gently removed the opened package, making sure not to spill any more of the valuable contents, and placed it on the table between David and me. David took a penknife from his pocket and proceeded to chop out a line on the tabletop and toot it. He sighed, turned to me and, smiling, said 'It's OK.'

What a relief. At least we finally knew that we had something worth travelling for, and now we had completed the outward stage we could turn our minds to getting it home. I was just about to hand the money to Jorge when he started rabbiting again, asking if we would give him some of the coke. Bloody crazy; we were in the middle of doing business and all this fool was concerned about was getting even more strung out in an alien city. Still, in the circumstances it was far easier to appease him than to argue, so I pulled a few grammes free from the package with David's penknife and slid them across the table. Jorge sat down and proceeded to chop out three lines. We refused ours and I slid the bundle of hundred-dollar bills across the table. Whilst Jorge sat and began to count the bundle of hundreds, I picked up my attaché case, opened it and from amongst the papers in it removed three large rolls of Elastoplast.

Time was of the essence now. It was three o'clock. God knows how far we were from the airport and I still had to strap David up. We worked quickly to reseal the one open package. David then stood up and stripped off his clothes, down to his underpants. The whole art of body packing is to spread it so that nothing pokes out or makes it uncomfortable for the wearer to move in a natural way. David lay face down on a single bed in the corner of the room and I laid three of the long, spaghetti-like packages lengthways across the middle of his back and taped them on. He then stood and we adjusted two more packets into the angles of his groin and taped them across. They would be very painful to remove, as the tape ran across the top of his pubic hair. The last packet to be taped on was the one Jorge had been helping himself to; it was a pain, as these packs are pressed under incredible pressure and once they are open they expand as air gets amongst the crystals of coke. After a great deal of pushing and prodding, we managed to arrange it across David's belly, above his waistline. I then proceeded to wrap him like a mummy with the remaining tape, pulling it as tight as possible without stopping his breathing. David got dressed and we examined our dressings. He looked OK and I figured as he only had to go through the metal scanner it would be fine.

We were ready to move and I turned to Jorge, who was having terrible trouble counting the money – he was so stoned he kept getting confused and having to start again. However, he was cool as he knew he would be able to head home tomorrow, collect his fee and start on his next trip and he did have a few grammes to keep him going. So David and I said our farewells and headed for the street and a cab to the airport.

The time was now 4.15 and we were really pushed. We started walking those monotonous suburban streets, looking for a cab. It was murder, as we had no idea which way the airport was and the streets were all so alike it was like being in a maze. During the walk, David was really uncomfortable and started talking of staying overnight and catching the first flight in the morning. But the truth was, I didn't have enough money for that and I really wanted to get this business done. Finally, at past 4.30, we hailed a cab. We both got in, and after thirty minutes of being snarled in Berlin's rush hour, we finally saw Tempelhof ahead. I felt like I had just found my way out of the jungle rather than simply making a jaunt across Berlin.

We composed ourselves as we climbed from the cab, although David did wince as the strapping caught his pubes. We'd agreed in the cab that we would separate as we entered the airport. David would go through customs first and I would hang back just in case they pulled him out – at least I would then be on the right side to help him.

After the check-in you went through an entrance that then hung a sharp right, so you couldn't see what happened at the customs from outside. I did not go through for ten minutes after David had entered and I only went then because they made the last call. If I could've turned back and left the airport without drawing suspicion as I turned the sharp right, I would've done so. There in front of me was a queue of people – not just going through a metal detector gate, as at Heathrow, but being patted down by a customs officer. I just don't know how I kept it together. I had by now got four or five people behind me and I couldn't just get out. I kept thinking of how lumpy and ridged the bindings of tape had looked when I had taped David up. I knew he couldn't have possibly got through a pat down. We just never thought that they would be doing individual pat downs in a European airport. I was going through and my mate must be in an interrogation cell downstairs. Had they seen me entering with him? Had they checked if anyone else had caught the same flight in, as well as out? Shit. How could I help if I was stuck on a flight to London? I was basically fucked.

I don't know how long I was in that queue, but it felt like eternity plus some; every bad option was going through my mind as I lifted my arms to be patted down. Then I was through to the departure lounge, but I knew as

I looked around that any second I would be leapt on, because I knew David couldn't have made it. I couldn't see him anywhere. Bollocks!

The public address was calling 'Last call for London'. I worked on automatic pilot and headed for the gate they were calling, all the time thinking, When are they going to jump me? What can I tell David's girlfriend? Everything was a mess, my mind was in turmoil, but I kept it together – just.

I had gone down the steps to the gate before I'd realised it and had obviously been lost in a welter of thought, as I bumped into the guy in front of me in the small queue to the sliding glass doors that lead to the steps up to the plane. I thought briefly about claiming that I'd left something and have to get out, or acting as if I was having a panic attack. In the end, though, I decided the best thing I could do was get back to London and do what I could for David from there, as there was fuck all I could do in Berlin with no money. By this time I was up the steps to the plane and was starting to believe that they hadn't sussed there were two of us. Small mercies.

I slumped into a seat near the front of the plane and prayed the damn thing would take off right then. They closed the door. Well, the only thing I had to worry about now was that they didn't phone ahead to London for me to be grabbed. At least I had an hour and a half to come up with some story to get them off my back. I would clear out my bag and make sure I had nothing on me with David's fingerprints on it. I had time and David had none.

The engines picked up and we trundled to the runway,

then they screamed and we were London-bound. I must have audibly sighed as we rose higher and higher and as we banked I looked down on the Berlin Wall; the wire made me think of my mate David banged up in some German holding cell. Damn!

Then the ping for seatbelt release came and I heard a voice shout: 'Can I get a drink now!'

I couldn't believe it. It was David. He had made it. The relief was palpable, I simply could not believe he could've got through. Then I was angry, really angry. We had agreed that we would make sure we were both through before boarding. But no, David clever dick had obviously decided to just wander through in his own time. The bastard. He didn't know just what grief he had put me through. I felt as if I had aged about twenty years in twenty minutes. It was a good job I couldn't go near him, or I would have knocked him out.

We landed at Heathrow on time. I went to the car park, collected my car and headed for our agreed rendezvous in Notting Hill. I was going against the rush hour and made it in half an hour, checking my mirror all the way for any surveillance and taking the back-doubles as I entered town. All was clear.

I walked into The Sun Inn Splendour and headed to the bar, where David was standing, knocking back a triple brandy. He saw me coming, turned towards me, and as I got close said: 'Let's go! This tape is fucking killing my pubes!'

I smiled to myself, then ordered another drink for him and one for myself. We might just stay for another hour. That would teach the bugger.

CHAPTER FOURTEEN

THE BIG ONE

A **COUPLE OF MONTHS** after the trip to Berlin, Coci called me and asked me over to Putney. He was extremely grateful for me getting Jorge out of a hole in October. I had a very nice lunch on him at the Caprice and we exchanged Christmas presents.

He told me the tale of the guy who had been popped in Berlin. It seems he had been arrested for being an illegal immigrant and had been deported. They weren't bothered by that. It was just very inconvenient that it happened the day Jorge was travelling there; in fact, the guy was back in Berlin on a different passport within two weeks.

Coci was being very friendly and told me that he was having problems in the States and was thinking of turning to Europe on a larger scale. He said that the guy in Berlin had found a good way of bringing goods in. He had found out by sheer coincidence when he had had some furniture shipped to him from Lima that freight goods to Berlin were shipped into East Berlin by some companies and then driven across into the West and the customs were never that bothered about these consignments. Coci thought that it would be a good way of getting stuff into Europe.

He was right. And if he could get goods into West Berlin, shipping them to anywhere else in Europe would be easy – the reason being that they would be thought to have originated from within Europe and thus far less likely to be scrutinised by customs, especially compared to anything shipped directly from Peru, which would be virtually certain of being opened and checked stringently.

I really liked the sound of this and told Coci that I would be into handling anything he wished to ship onward into England; I also reminded him of the positive price advantage in England.

Coci told me the method he was going to use; it was even better than I had thought. He had access to a metal foundry in Peru and they were already casting truck wheels in which the axle spindles were cast separately; 2 to 4 kilos were wrapped around them and then they were dropped into place and welded in. It was a beautiful method, as it had two lovely extra qualities. One: the coke would not show up if X-rayed. Two: as the wheels had the axle holes running all the way through, the customs would be able to see right through and give them the illusion of having seen inside. I thought it was brilliant. Coci said they had never been tumbled going into the States. It was the people there who were giving him grief and that was why he was considering Europe. We left it that he would do a trial run into Berlin in the next couple of months and let me know how he got on.

There was only one disappointing aspect to come out of the lunch and that was that the two Americans who had been bringing in the wall hangings had decided to retire. So that was the end of that scam and made my hopes for the success of the trial of the truck wheels even greater.

After that, Mary and I went off to the Gazelle D'Or in Taradount, Morocco, for Christmas. It was then a secret place that hadn't become a feature on the tourist map. We relaxed in the tranquil surroundings and life was exceptionally good. The only trouble was the other guests: they were all hoorays and ex-colonials, who adopted a nasty attitude towards the Moroccan staff. Why do the English feel such a need to adopt a superior attitude to others? I always think it only shows their inferiority. Still, we had a lovely time amidst the palms, eating some of the loveliest food imaginable. The most exotic pleasure was the breakfasts, carried on a huge silver tray to your bungalow on the shoulder of a waiter and consisting of the freshest orange pressé, coffee and the lightest brioche and croissants made by human hand.

Mary spent the whole time in the Hamman (Turkish bath to you) being pummelled and pampered. Southern Morocco is fabulous at that time of year. You have lovely warm days and cold, even frosty nights. Delicious, as at the Gazelle D'Or after a fab dinner in a magnificent dining room you go back to your bungalow to find a roaring log fire has been lit in your absence. Trés bloody romantique if you ask me. Well, it was for us. Regenerated, we returned to grey England, ready for what was to be a memorable year.

The company was bombing along now. I was up and out to work at four or five o'clock most days and so I never had much time to worry about whether Coci's trial would happen or not. I only thought about it when I was scoring coke for myself, as this was the first time in years that I had to be a punter. Even if I was getting it from friends who were close to the importation and thus ensured good quality, I really got pissed off at having to pay full price. Well, nearly full price.

The tensions in the company were getting a bit much at this time. Eddie really was taking the piss with his poncing about rather than working. Everyone was fed up with him. I should have done more about it, but I just tried to calm things down, as I doubted whether there was any point in trying to change his attitude.

Come April, we had our books done and I was a bit shocked to find that after all the work we'd put in that we hadn't made any money. Eddie was the reason, as he milked the company for what he could get out of it. It was a shame, because it was a good business and if he had realised that he would just have to wait a bit for the good times, we would have cracked it in a year or two. However you couldn't talk to him about it.

I was probably still too cash rich to toughen up and let things run. Also, I was really enjoying being involved in a straight business without having to live with the permanent paranoia of having to watch my rear-view mirror wherever I went. It also made things a lot easier at home as Mary was always going on at me to stop scamming. She has always been more aware of the dangers than me and was constantly going on at me about it. So I was very keen for the business to work out even if, money-wise, I was hoping for Coci's test run to work.

The whole business of my marriage and involvement in scamming is a difficult one for me to write about. My wife enjoyed the money but she was never mercenary and her concern about my involvement shouldn't be seen as wanting the best of both worlds. She really was worried that if I was busted I'd be gone for a long time. I sometimes said she was being unfair, but the truth was I knew what she meant and I just didn't want to hear it. I had made my choices and the only way you can stay involved is by ignoring the dangers – if you don't, you just can't function, as you would be a total nervous wreck whenever you went anywhere holding anything. I don't believe it's being an ostrich – you have to be aware, just not all the time.

So I was enjoying freedom from the constraints of being a dealer and finding it very nice. Then, in May, Coci was back in town and it was scam big-time. The test run had gone with absolutely no problems, so we sat in a bar in Putney and talked of how we were going to get 100 kilos at a time into England. That is, at wholesale, approximately £2.5 million worth. A lot of money and of that I was to make £0.5 million. I had thought about how to go about it and I reckoned it would be relatively easy. The big joy of the whole thing was that it was to be on credit, as there was no way I could have afforded to have paid up front for that sort of amount.

I had only three problems to overcome. They were: firstly, that Coci wanted it moved much faster than I could handle at that time and although I wasn't very happy about it I would have to bring in someone else or Coci wouldn't give it to me. Secondly, I would need a proper stash in which to unpack and hide it. I had the catering company yard, but that was to close to home and I didn't think I could trust Eddie and Fatboy if they knew I had those sort of quantities around. Thirdly, I needed to find a shipping agent who would monitor the goods for any surveillance by the authorities and also, as it was rather a shaky receiving company I would have to set up, it would be so much easier if the agents were on-side.

I spent a few weeks thinking of renting a yard and of who I could approach re an agent, as well as the biggest problem of all – that of finding more outlets. It's not the sort of franchise you can advertise in the Daily Mail. I was getting very concerned, as I knew that I wouldn't be able to meet the commitment I had made with Coci if I couldn't resolve these issues quickly. Then the solution came along through pure serendipity.

I was buying some flowers in Battersea one day and I met an old friend of Mick's called Terry, whom I hadn't seen for ages. I knew he had worked with Mick before he'd gone to Amsterdam. I had seen him for Mick and had done a few things with him at that time, and I remembered Mick telling me one time that he had someone involved with a shipping company, but we hadn't seen one another for a few years, so I wasn't sure how things were now. I knew he was part of an old South London family and that he owned a building company based in Lambeth, but not a lot more. We stood in Battersea Park Road talking of this and that, when he asked me out of the blue if I could get him some coke. I thought this might be another outlet, so we went for a bacon sarnie and a chat.

Over the next couple of weeks we did some business, and as it went on I realised that he was a perfect partner for this scam. He had a yard in Lambeth where I went to drop off a couple of times. It was perfect for a stash being secure, and he was only using it as an office with no one else being there. Also, he appeared to be able to move a fair amount as he had taken a few kilos over those weeks.

Terry was very different from me in that he was straight and didn't take any drugs. The only worry was that his connections were all villains from what I could gather, and I had always avoided villains like the plague. I was used to working with old hippies like myself and was very nervous of involving Terry's connections as they seemed to be so up front and in the cops' faces. Then I figured that I was just being irrational, as the truth was I didn't really know any villains and I had only formed opinions based on second-hand info.

So one evening I went for a drink with Terry, told him the basics of the scam and asked him if he wanted to become involved. Of course, he said yes and agreed to the use of his yard for unpacking and stashing. He also told me that he had someone who would act as the importing agents – for a fee, of course. I didn't bother to ask about his distribution, as we were already doing business together.

I was really chuffed at my luck. I hadn't spoken to Coci for a month or so, which was fortunate for me, as until my confab with Terry I really wasn't in a position to be able to carry out my end of the scam. Once that meeting had resolved the basics, we were able to sort out the fake company and the shipping agents within a week. Then I was waiting for Coci. Robbie was still around and I got him to phone Peru, but Coci wasn't about. All I could do was sit and wait.

Well, not so much sit, as the catering company was really busy. By now it was summer and we were out on location all the time. It was so odd to be working my butt off with the company and having the scam forever in my mind. You just had to keep the two areas totally separate and carry on as normal, waiting and waiting for that call. Finally, at the end of July, Coci rang and I was off to Putney. Funnily enough, although this scam was the largest I was to be involved in, I never felt any pressure until the end. The reason was that I was not involved physically in the importation and by this time the selling of the coke had become such a habit to me that it was no different to running any other business. I was always aware of being illegal, but the adrenaline only got running occasionally on this one. Well, as I said, until the end.

Coci was full of the joys, as he had a shipment sitting in Berlin waiting to come over. Inevitably though, there was a problem: there were only 20 kilos. I was pissed, as I had negotiated a fixed price with the shipping agents based on 100 kilos of £20,000 for their monitoring services. So I would have to go back and renegotiate, which I knew would be difficult as they would be suspicious that I was trying to have them over. Also, I had brought Terry in on the basis that I needed him and was splitting my profit with him. With a consignment of only 20 kilos, I could have done it all on my own. However there was no way I could start again now that the goods were in Berlin ready for shipping. Anyway, I would still make £90,000 on the 20 kilos – it really wasn't enough, but I figured that if this one went OK we would start shipping on a regular basis.

The only other problem I had sounds minor but it was the most difficult to deal with. I had promised Mary that we would go to Greece during the summer holidays for a month. We were due to leave in ten days and I dreaded telling her that I wouldn't be able to go. Crazy, but I was more worried about this than the possibility of anything going wrong with the actual scam. I decided the only way to not worry her was to tell her I was working on location and would come a week later. I figured I could have everything cleared and the money delivered within a week of the coke's arrival.

The next week went quickly. We sent off the order from the accommodation address we were using in Mayfair and waited for the confirmation from Berlin. The office service received that confirmation by the Friday and the coke left the same day. The shipping agents were told to expect the consignment on the Monday or Tuesday.

I remember spending that weekend trying to act as if nothing was happening. We went to stay with some friends in Brighton. As we walked the front I watched some container ships passing up the Channel and wondered if any of them contained my truck wheels with the 20 kilos of cocaine. Of course, they didn't, but I smiled at the thought, crossed the road to the Grand and ordered champagne and proceeded to have a grand night. I just knew that the shipment would get through.

* * *

The Monday morning came and I was booked out on location for the next three days. We even had one of the first mobiles – which were more like a brick than anything mobile – on our truck, so I could be reached if necessary. However, we weren't expecting the wheels to arrive until Tuesday or Wednesday, and we wanted to leave them for a day to see if any observations were going on. I carried on humping food around a muddy field all that day and the next. Then, late on the Tuesday, Terry called and I popped into his yard on my way home from work. He told me that they had arrived and everything seemed OK. He had arranged that the shipping agents would drop them off early on the Thursday.

I carried on working for the Wednesday, didn't sleep much that night and was up and out at 5.30 a.m. I then drove up to Smithfield Market and had some breakfast, checking all the time to see if I was being watched. I saw nothing. So after a wander around the market, I headed back down to Lambeth and reached the yard by 8 a.m.; Terry was already there when I arrived and we sat drinking coffee for half an hour. Then a truck pulled into the yard. It was here.

We went out and the driver's first words were: 'Where's your forklift?' Oops! We never realised the wheels were for a 10-ton lorry. They must have weighed about 100 kilos each, there were two to a crate and the crates were big. Madness.

Terry and I struggled to get the five crates off the lorry. I still can't believe we didn't get hernias or have heart attacks shifting them. Thank God there weren't the twenty-five crates that 100 kilos would have required; we would have dropped dead before having unloaded them.

We managed to finally get them off and into the workshop and the driver went off laughing. As he left the yard we slapped one another on the back and collapsed onto the floor in laughter ourselves.

I sat panting, looking at those crates, which were open-slated with the wheels sitting in them, and thinking to myself that they were truly a stroke of genius. You could see the wheels in the crates and you could see right through the axles, everything was exposed, nothing looked hidden in any way. They were wonderful; but I was buggered.

After half an hour we had got ourselves together and started the unpacking. It was easy, we wedged a wheel and gave its centre a whack with a big sledgehammer. The centre popped out, looking just like a giant cotton reel, though it was wrapped with packs of coke, not thread. Very nice. We had the wheels knocked out and the coke weighed up in an hour and everything was fine. My premonition in Brighton had been right.

I found the whole thing very strange, though, as I had none of that pumping adrenaline that had gone with previous scams. I suppose it was partially overfamiliarity and partially that it was delivered to my doorstep. It really was an excellent take-away service. All we needed now was for it to become regular.

Clearing the coke only took a week and by the following Friday I was sitting in my car outside a hotel in Kensington with two Sainsbury's bags containing £300,000, waiting for Coci. It was so funny: I had promised to get some food out to a location site in time for lunch and I was running late. So instead of being paranoid about what I was doing I was more concerned about getting on my way to deliver food for forty starving people – a reflection of how confusing the overlaps between the two worlds could become at times.

Coci came out of the hotel and we went for a drive around to discuss what we would do next. He told me that he wanted to do more, but that there were problems in Peru with the Americans. They were sponsoring a big push against the factories in the jungle and we would have to wait until after Christmas before doing any more. I was happy with this, as I felt that a long break would allow any heat, if there was any, to cool off.

I drove back to the hotel and Coci went to get out of the car. As he lifted the carrier bags out the handle went on one of them, and about £150,000 in bundles fell out onto the pavement. A woman walking by glanced, walked on and then turned and looked back in amazement as she realised what she'd seen. I felt as if the whole world was watching a bank robbery as Coci threw the bundles back into the car and we pulled away rather quickly. That was the only paranoia I felt in the whole of that scam, but it was quite enough.

Oh, and I got *such* a bollocking from the producer of the commercial at the location when I turned up late with lunch.

CHAPTER FIFTEEN

A WELL-EARNED BREAK

TERRY AND I had only sold enough of the coke to pay Coci off but we weren't too worried as we could now take our time selling the rest and make a larger profit. We intended to sell four of the kilos in ounces, therefore upping the return to £35,000 rather than the £25,000 if we sold each kilo wholesale. Doing this would enable us to cover the £20,000 that the shipping agents had insisted upon, even though the amount was 20 kilos not 100, and still add £20,000 to our profit. Mr Happy was wearing a big smile.

Moreover, with Coci not wanting to attempt another big one until after Christmas '87, we had plenty of time to slowly knock it out. We sold the 4 kilos we wanted to wholesale and from that £100,000 we paid off the agents and had £40,000 each left in cash.

So we were off for our month in Greece. I had done the business with two days to spare so in the end I didn't have to upset Mary and say I'd leave later. We packed our company jeep and headed for France and the grand tour to Greece.

You don't want a travelogue, so just let it be said Lausanne, Lake Como, Florence and Nauphlion could not have been better when Byron travelled through. The island of Siros, where we spent three weeks, was a million miles from the world of drugs and money, as you can imagine; I wandered the island looking for land to buy and build on.

My friend Percy, who ran the house of Sir Richard Musgrave that was used in Octopussy, was on good form.

We all had a glorious time together on a wonderful beach called Delphini, to which no more than twenty people came each day. Perfection. We returned after an extensive shopping trip to Florence and Paris rested and ready for more good times.

While I was away I decided to invest the money from the wheels into a large new truck for the catering company. It was something Eddie had asked me to consider and I thought there was no reason not to. The new truck was to be a state-of-the-art mobile office in one half and a wardrobe and make-up department in the other. My brother, a designer, did a great job with it. The only problem was, it took eight months from buying the shell to finishing it. However, come June '87, it was on the road and everyone loved it. The fact that it cost £60,000 didn't bother me, as I was genuinely pleased to think I was investing in a company that was growing.

We moved the company to a yard in Vauxhall, not ten minutes from Terry's yard. This was pure coincidence, but it was very handy. The business just seemed to grow, we took on more people and it was still great fun to go out on location. I was able to do my coke business in just a few hours a week. The people whom I supplied were all very close and had their own close customers, so no one was out there looking for new business. It just rolled along quietly and smoothly.

Mary and I had our close friends and we would be out most weekends at some do or other. We got into the habit of going to some country hotel or restaurant on a Sunday for lunch with our mates. All in all, we had a great time of it, although I'm not sure everyone enjoyed the way I drove back to London from Oxford or the New Forest.

The thing was, that although we had as much money as we wanted, we weren't hanging out in flash clubs and restaurants and being noticed. We had a very stable group of mates and although I was providing the drugs, everyone was a friend. We never tolerated liggers and we were never looking to make new friends at the openings and first nights we attended. It was, very simply, a very nice life.

The only downside going on at that time was my old friend David – who was the only one of the original four that went to Morocco that I still saw – was into smack in a bad way. He had moved to the country with his wife and kids and was running his carpet business from there. However, he was way over the top and his marriage was on the rocks. It hard for me to contemplate, as I had introduced him to his wife, who had worked for me when I ran the clothes shops a few years earlier. He had always been crazy and dabbled with smack off and on, but now he was way past the dabbling stage. He would come to town and stay in the Chelsea Arts Club and had become notorious for nodding out and being stroppy in the bar there. Bad news indeed.

One week he came to stay with us in Battersea intent on cleaning up. So he said. My father was in town and coming to meet me for a drink before going off to some wine trade function, so I came home to wait for him. I walked in to find David chasing the dragon on the mantelpiece; as I started to go berserk, the doorbell went. It was my old man. This I didn't need. I dragged David into the spare bedroom and opened the windows before letting the old man in. I don't think he noticed anything, but who knows.

The next day I decided to take David to Dorset and Clouds, to see if he would go in there for a cure. We drove down and I remember walking in to the sound of clapping coming from a group applauding someone's soul-cleansing. I left him to talk it through with a counsellor and returned an hour later. He asked to go to the pub to talk it over. After we had got a drink we sat outside the pub and I'll never forget him saying to me, 'I bet you wouldn't stay there.' 'Yeah, but I'm not the one fucked up,' I replied.

Anyway, the upshot was that I paid for a month and I left him there. Four days later, he rang to say he had escaped. He broke his back in a car crash in December '88. David lived on, a crazy and awkward bastard in a wheelchair, and died in March 2001. A sad loss of a great friend.

Other than David, everything seemed to go so well up to Christmas '87. In the run up to Christmas, I also met a very useful connection. I had been thinking about getting the cash from the next consignment out of the country and it was a bit of a worry. Sending it through the banking system was very difficult, because of the government checks on large cash transfers that the Thatcher government had implemented and the thought of £2.5 million being carried out was a worry, even if we stashed it in a car or van. Then, through Robbie, I met an enigmatic New Yorker named Stephen.

Robbie used to go to the Groucho quit a bit at that time. He had met Stephen there, and they had become good mates. One night we were out with Robbie and he introduced us. Stephen was a great guy, a bit too into hookers for me, but very funny and good company, if a little too misogynistic for Mary; we got on really well that night, though.

Over the next few weeks, I had lunch with him and Robbie a few times and it slowly came out that he was involved in some big American insurance scam. I let on what my business was; somehow it came out that he was getting large amounts of Swiss francs into England, but needed sterling and was having difficulties in changing it up. This was really good news for me, as not only was he getting the francs, but they were in 1,000-franc notes and at the time each note was worth about £300. This meant that you could carry £1 million worth in your pockets at a squeeze. I was really pleased at this lucky encounter – not only for business, but because Stephen became a very close friend. He lives in Southeast Asia now and has a string of very successful restaurants down there.

Then Christmas came and we were off to Morocco again, to have another great time. I was hoping to have heard from Coci by now, but I knew I would just have bide my time.

CHAPTER SIXTEEN

THE BEGINNING OF THE END

WE CAME BACK from Morocco on January 2, 1988 in great shape. Then, a week into the new year, Coci rang.

I went to meet him at his friend's place in Putney as usual and he said he would definitely be sending 50 kilos in the wheels in the spring and every six months after that. I was over the moon, as that would mean I would make half a million in the next year. Life was sweet. The next two months flew by and before I knew it Coci was back. It was March and spring was showing its beauty in Battersea Park as he and I walked and talked in the sunshine. Everything was in place; he had the stuff packed and ready to go as soon as he returned to Peru.

The only change was that he didn't want to collect the money himself. He admitted the reason was that he made a policy of not being around when the business was actually going on, which was perfectly sensible and I definitely didn't want him around if anything did go wrong. He asked if I could arrange to transfer the money to Miami through a bank in the UK. I told him that paying large amounts of cash into British banks was an absolute no-no as the government had introduced very strict regulations on the monitoring of such deposits, and that under no circumstances could any of the cash be deposited in the UK.

I then told him about Stephen and the Swiss francs – something that he was really pleased to hear about. He said in that case he would send a relative of his named Martha, who was married to an Englishman who lived in Peru, to collect the cash. We agreed he would bring her over the week before the shipment was due, to introduce us. And off he went. The only thing Terry and I had to do now was buy a forklift, as neither of us fancied lifting those crates manually again. So Terry went out and bought a second-hand one.

Come the middle of April, Coci was back with Martha, who was fine. I did worry that she looked too Peruvian, but she was a nice woman so I left it at that. We agreed a specific date and hotel for her to come to at the end of May to collect the money. Coci said that was fine, as she would be collecting money in Berlin at the same time, and told me to send the order off to Germany the next day.

A week later Terry and I were sitting in his yard after a hard morning's unpacking, surrounded by what looked like fifty bags of sugar. The only difference was that these bags were worth £1.25 million and £0.5 million of it was ours. It was the last week of April and that meant we had a month to sell 30 kilos in order to sort Coci out. No problem, we said. If only.

I still don't know why, but I was only able to sell 8 kilos to my people in the next month and Terry only sold one. I couldn't moan, but he didn't have the outlets that I'd thought he had. We were in trouble. I had promised to give Martha £0.75 million when she came, and all I had managed to scrape together when I went to meet her was £0.25 million. In retrospect, this was the beginning of the nightmare.

I had tried to contact Coci to tell him of my problem before going to meet Martha, but I had no luck with his friends in Putney and Robbie couldn't raise him through his friends in Peru. He had disappeared. So I had no choice but to go and meet Martha, give her what I had and get her to tell Coci to contact me. I met her, gave her the money and she was cool. I asked her where the money was going as I wanted to be absolutely sure that she was not going to deposit any of the money in Britain and she said Coci had told her to take all of it to Miami. That was good news and I told her to return in a month. Hopefully, we would be sorted out by then. Finally, I asked her if she would she please get Coci to contact me.

I spent the next few days desperately trying to get things moving more quickly, but it didn't happen and you can't go out and shout that you have got 20 kilos of coke to sell. I was also very busy with the catering company and it was a nightmare trying to work at a job while trying to speed things up on the coke front.

Then, a week after she had left, I got a call from Martha. She was staying with the guys in Putney. I went over to see her, with only £50,000. When I got there I suddenly found myself being harangued by her and the gay South American guy about the balance of the money. It was murder, because they had no idea of how the business worked and I had no way of talking to them in a logical way. I asked again for Coci to contact me, but they told me he wasn't willing to come and it ended with Martha saying she would come every week until the money was paid. I went ballistic – the thought of her flying in and out every week was a nightmare. A Peruvian national coming into

London so regularly was inevitably going to draw attention. However, she would not wait a month and, sure enough, every week until the end of June I had her phoning from some hotel and having to go and drop what I had. Over that time I gave her a total of £0.25 million.

At the end of June, I went to meet her and this time she had her English husband with her. He was a pain. He was trying to impress as some sort of latter-day ex-colonial but again, I could not get through to them that they would have to wait and let me contact them when I had all the money. However, they just wouldn't listen and said one or the other of them would return the following week.

They didn't come the next week, which I thought was weird. Still, when the husband called the second week of July I was OK, because I had the last £0.25 million for them. I went to meet him feeling overjoyed, safe in the knowledge that it would be the last time I would have to see them; they had driven me mad for the previous two months and at last I was going to be rid of them. I drove to the hotel feeling really good, but was careful as usual, checking I wasn't being followed. I gave Martha's husband the money, told him I didn't want to see him or his wife again and asked him to get Coci to ring me.

I walked out of the hotel feeling a great weight had been lifted off of me and couldn't prevent a smile crossing my face. Then, as I pulled away, I noticed a car pull out a few cars back. I hung an illegal right at the next set of lights, just as a safety measure. If it was them, they were likely to do the same illegal turn. Bollocks – the car did the same. I didn't like it, so I went for a little drive, and sure enough I was being followed. I knew straight away that Martha, her husband, or both of them had been sussed at the airport and they were onto them and now me. Nightmare time. We still had 20 kilos and I was under observation.

I didn't try to get rid of the tail, as I didn't want them to know I had sussed them. So I drove home and went for a walk and a think in Battersea park – with two guys following me at a discreet distance. Not nice. But don't panic!

My first thoughts were positive. At least Martha and her husband wouldn't be a problem, as this was their last visit and as long as they didn't bust them at the airport on their way out they would be out of the equation. I had nothing around me at home and I was sure they didn't know about Terry. I decided that I would just act normal, and that Mary and I would head off to Greece for a month and let everything go cold. I had £10,000 in cash stashed, so I had no need to rush and sell my share of the coke; I decided to stop for a few months.

I walked back to our flat with my two new friends attached to me as if by invisible elastic. I went in and checked that there wasn't anything incriminating there – there wasn't. The two things I still had to do was meet Terry to tell him the situation and to contact my distributors without my new friends knowing. I figured it would be better sooner rather than later – I presumed they wouldn't have a team on me yet, as I was convinced they had only just picked up on me at the hotel meeting.

Luckily, our mansion block of flats had two back entrances, so I walked across the back yard, which couldn't be seen from outside, came out on the next road and wandered off. I knew straight away that I was clean. I had slipped them. I walked off into the back streets of Battersea to a phone box I knew that was tucked away and spent fifteen minutes phoning my people and telling them not to ring me under any circumstances. Then I arranged to meet Terry fifteen minutes later in a place that we both knew we could get to and be sure we weren't being followed.

We found ourselves standing on a bridge across the main Waterloo–Clapham junction line, watching for any unusual walkers or cars. We weren't paranoid enough to be looking for helicopters, but we were definitely watchful. There wasn't much to say. I knew I had to go away and Terry agreed. We decided to meet in the same place eight weeks later at a certain time and to have no contact whatsoever unless something really drastic happened.

There was only one other thing that I felt needed to be done, and that was regarding the accommodation address. When I had registered with them, I had to fill out a form and although I had used a false name and address and disguised my handwriting as well as I could, I felt it would be best if that form was destroyed.

In retrospect, I should have gone in and just asked for it using some excuse, such as needing it for tax purposes or the like. However, during my walk in the park, I decided to ask Terry if he could get someone to burgle the place and destroy it. The last thing I asked Terry was whether he could arrange the burglary – he said he would. After that, I left him and made my way back towards the flat, musing on my concerns regarding the Peruvians.

I had no idea what was happening with Coci or Martha and in a way, although I was concerned, I felt it safer not to know. I figured I was clean with regard to them, as long as Martha hadn't been busted on her way out with the money, as that could be the only evidence connecting us. As long as I wasn't pulled in the next few days, I could presume she had got clean away and that I would not have to worry about her.

As far as the importation was concerned, I figured we couldn't be busted for that, as it had been done; there was no documentation to connect me with Germany, as I had disposed of every bit of it except for the registration document, but hopefully Terry was arranging the loss of that.

The big problem was what was happening to the South Americans. Therefore, I would have to go and see Coci's gay friend in Putney. I figured that he was the only loose link in the UK. Even if he wasn't involved, he knew who I was and I didn't know if Coci or Martha had ever left my phone number, or anything else pertaining to me, with him. Moreover, if they had been followed there at any time, then he may well get a visit. More importantly, he was the only contact I had to Coci that would enable me to tell him to keep away and to find out whether anything had happened in Germany or Peru.

I would have to leave it for a few days, but I really worried that he might contact me in the interim if anything had happened to the others – if they were tapping my phone, it could cause problems. However, I figured I would simply say he'd got a wrong number if he did ring, as that was safer than going to see him for the moment.

As I neared the flat, I figured that I had covered everything. Then I realised I had a more immediate problem: I couldn't go in my front door, as obviously my followers – if they were still there – would know I'd been out. But I didn't have a key to the gate I had come out of. How was I to get back in? I had to climb the gate and I thought as I did, that it would be a bitch if I was caught and had to explain myself.

I told myself everything would be fine and was sitting reading the paper when Mary came in full of the joys and ready for an evening out that we'd arranged with some friends. I said nothing. I just didn't want her upset – and what good would it do, anyway? I had thought of saying I was going to leave the country on my own for a few months, but I knew this would totally freak her, and I couldn't leave her on her own. I knew she wouldn't want to go on the run like that – plus, she had her job to think of. So I carried on as if everything was normal. We went out that night as planned, and my two friends had gone. I knew they hadn't gone permanently though – they'd be back. Sure enough, over the next three weeks I was picked up and followed at random times.

One day was sheer hysteria. The bank for the company was in Peckham and I had to go and pay in some cheques, as we wanted the funds cleared as quickly as possible. It was a tail day, but believe me, I didn't set out to cause them problems. It was just that the best route from Kings Cross to Peckham involved some very twisty backstreet manoeuvring, and I was genuinely in a hurry to get back to the yard for a delivery.

I shot out of the yard at a fair old lick and we were off on one. The car that had followed me to work shot out with a squeal of tyres; I had obviously surprised them. I won't bore you with the details, so I'll just fast-forward half an hour and five minutes from the bank and a quiet little dead-end street in Peckham, which I had mistakenly turned into due to a combination of being caught up with watching my followers and rushing to make the bank.

Of course, the only way I could get out of the dead end was to turn around, and as I did so (and I don't exaggerate) a convoy of three saloon cars, a BT van, a white transit, three mopeds and a motorbike all turned into the road. The looks on their faces as I drove back past them was a joy. They knew that I knew at that point – though the trouble was, I didn't want them to know that I knew. Never mind, it made me smile and that was a relief at the time, even if it was for just a moment. They must have been pissed, though, because all I usually did was go to work and come home again.

I write this very matter-of-factly but although I was feeling comfortable while just going to work, the morning

I had decided to go to Putney I was stressed – very stressed. It seems such an ordinary thing to go to Putney and ring a doorbell, but if they were watching, or if they had already raided that flat, the consequences could be devastating. Knowing that every move I made could be watched was nerve-wracking. And what of my car? I figured it could have a bug fitted after the fiasco in Peckham, but I couldn't check and remove it if there was one. So I definitely couldn't go to Putney by car.

I thought my best plan was to drive off in my car, head towards the yard in Kings Cross, make sure I wasn't being closely followed. Then I would leave it near a tube station, catch a tube, do a few changes to make sure I wasn't followed and then walk from Putney station to the flat.

I knew that wouldn't cover what might have already happened there, but that was something I couldn't plan for. I would just have to ring and hope nothing was wrong. Of course, the other thing was, would he be there after all that?

So a little stress was definitely buzzing around as I set off at 6 a.m. Why at that time? Two reasons. Firstly, it would be easier to check for a tail. Secondly, I figured if I got to Putney by 8 a.m. I would be more likely to find him home. I drove checking everything moving on the road, including joggers and dogs. I thought I was clear by the time I got to Kings Cross station, parked and ran for the tube. Three-quarters of an hour and several changes of tube later, I was walking out of Putney station feeling I was safe from being followed at least. Now I only had to worry about the response to my ringing the doorbell of the flat.

I must confess, I was shaking a bit as I walk down the road to that flat thinking they were watching me as I approached. I almost turned and ran, but I figured I'd come this far, so what the fuck. I walked past the flat, checked cars and windows, then turned and made for the house. I opened the gate and, with heart pumping, walked up the path half expecting someone to jump out and grab me.

I rang the top bell and waited. Nothing. I rang again for longer this time. Then I jumped as I heard a noise. It was a window opening. There, looking down and half-asleep, was Coci's friend. 'I'll come down,' he called. I sighed with relief as the tension lifted. They hadn't been there.

He made me a cup of tea and we talked.

'I spoke to Martha last week and she was just leaving Germany and everything was fine,' he told me.

That was a relief. I told him of my being under observation after leaving Martha and that he must contact Coci to close everything down for six months and to make sure that everyone (including him) disposed of any numbers or paperwork of any kind.

He was rattled now and I knew that if he was ever questioned, he would be useless. Still, he said agreed to do what I had asked and I left. I travelled back to get my car feeling relieved that everything seemed OK. I figured that Martha must have simply attracted attention to us by all her trips to England. Everything would be alright now though, as whoever it was watching me had got onto it too late and as long as I just carried on as normal, they would give up and go away eventually.

So that was how things stood two weeks later, when it came time for us to leave for the drive to Greece. I was shitting myself as we went into Dover harbour, thinking that if they were going to stop me it would be then. Nothing happened, though, and we were off.

The next five weeks were great. I relaxed and thought things through. I decided over many a quiet ouzo while Mary lay sunbathing that I couldn't face the possibility of trouble from my mysterious shadows and decided to quit. I had a nice home and a good business that was growing; the £0.25 million could go into property and we would be fine.

I decided that if everything was cool on my return I would give my 10 kilos to someone to sell off instead of doing it slowly myself. I could make between £50,000 and £100,000 more if I did it myself, but I figured £0.25 million was enough. The guy I had in mind to give it to was someone I had never worked with – Alan Stanton, who was the boyfriend of our old friend Mona. Pat, the guy whom I'd had the security company with, and Mona's ex-boyfriend had mentioned him to me a few months before in a conversation and had told me what a nice and reliable guy he was.

The island we went to on our trips is Siros. It is a beautiful island that is mainly used by Greeks, and it's wonderful. We had made some very good friends there and my old friend Percy Raines, whom I had known since The Speakeasy in the Sixties, was a butler to a family who had a magnificent house on the island. We were really close – Mary and I loved Percy and whenever we were there we talked of buying a place of our own. On this trip, Mary and I went and looked at ten or fifteen houses and pieces of land, but I couldn't risk buying anything until I had sorted things at home.

Percy had found a house he wanted to buy, but he didn't have enough money for it, so he asked me to lend him the balance. He promised to pay it back or share the house with us. This seemed a really good move, and so I lent him the cash when he was in London later in the year.

It seems funny to me now the way I was able to go on completely normally, all the while worrying about all the possibilities that could be waiting for me on my return. But I did, and although I was tense coming back through Dover the first week of September, I felt OK.

CHAPTER SEVENTEEN

BUSTED

MY FEELING THAT everything was fine seemed justified the first week we were back. I was watching everybody and everything wherever I went. I saw nothing and I heard from no one, so I figured everything was OK.

Then, a week after my return, I got the call that I didn't want. The guy in Putney called and said he had to see me; I said I'd see him in the park by Putney Bridge. An hour later we were walking by the river and I got the bad news. It seemed that the guy in Germany who had run the company there and had shipped on to me had had his flat busted the first week in August. There was good news, though. After my warning, he had left Germany and everyone else was safe in Peru. When I asked, he said there was nothing incriminating in the Berlin flat.

Then he dropped the bombshell that totally freaked me. Martha had been stopped every single time she had left the UK. I couldn't believe that she had never bothered to even mention it to me. It seemed that they found the money every time as well. However, she hadn't told me about it as they let her go! God, how stupid can you get?

Anyway, although I was pissed, from what he said it seemed that the authorities had missed the boat, and I figured they would only be interested in me as someone to keep an eye on in future. As long as I did quit, things would be fine. I told the guy to get rid of anything with my name or numbers on and never to contact me again. I then turned and walked away, thinking that that would be the last I would see of the Peruvians for a long time.

The shadows didn't seem to be following me any more, so I figured they must have realised that they had missed the boat, especially as they had hit the flat in Berlin but hadn't come near me. I had escaped by the skin of my teeth and everything was going to be fine. Well, in theory – I knew it wasn't as clear cut as that. If they had known about the money and Martha and had hit the Berlin flat, they must've had something. I wracked my brain, but there were so many questions that it was impossible to come to any coherent answer. The only conclusion I was left with was that I had to quit and I had to get my 10 kilos laid off with someone as soon as possible.

The walk by the river was a nasty surprise and although I was working on location and trying to stop myself getting too distracted, I was stressed. I wasn't sleeping properly and getting pretty ratty. I don't think I was aware of it at the time, but in retrospect I was under a lot of pressure.

After that meeting, I decided to tell Eddie Cowell of my worries and to sort out an agreement as to what we would do if I was ever busted. I had put something like £150,000 into the company over the years and felt that I must have some agreement with him as to what he would give Mary if the worst were to happen.

So, the day after the Putney meeting, I sat down with him and he happily agreed that if anything were to happen he would give Mary £1,000 a month for three years and then we would negotiate again. Of course, he was very happy with this arrangement, as it was extremely beneficial to him – it would only mean a repayment of £36,000 on my investment of approximately £150,000. I remember him saying, 'Don't worry Bob I'd never let you down. Anyway I don't think anything will happen from what you've told me.'

A few days after the meeting in Putney, I decided to sort out the placing of my 10 kilos – I had to have it sorted before seeing Terry, as arranged, before going to Greece. I wanted to be able to make that meeting our last for a long time.

The pressure seemed to be unrelenting in the days after the meeting in Putney. I couldn't stop turning the unanswered questions over and over in my mind, with no resolution. Although I felt uncomfortable, and was constantly on the lookout for being followed, I still felt I had to get the 10 kilos placed somewhere outside of my circle as soon as possible, particularly as my meeting with Terry was due to take place the following week.

It was crazy, as I was going against all my precepts of not being involved with people I hadn't known since the year dot. Still, I went ahead and rang Pat my old partner from the security company from a phone box, arranging to meet him in The Windmill pub on Clapham Common.

We walked on the common while his Ridgeback tried to kill every other dog there, and between sorting out screaming dog owners I told him of my problem. I asked Pat whether he thought Mona's new boyfriend Alan, the guy he had told me about before I had gone to Greece, was a good guy. Pat told me Alan was very busy in the business and assured me that he was totally genuine and reliable. I asked him to arrange a meeting the next day at the same place.

You couldn't help but like Alan. He was not a handsome man. He was small, fat and had the round red face of a serious drinker, with nicotine stained fingers, but there was a humour in his face that was very infectious. The fact he had a vague resemblance to Charlie Drake the comic probably gave me an unconscious predisposition to like him – weird, really, as I never liked Charlie Drake. He was a villain through and through, but he had a charm that drew me in. I was totally up-front about my situation with him and about what I was considering doing.

We talked of the drugs business and during the conversation a few names came up that turned out to be mutual associates. A small world, drug-dealing. That was perfect, as it would enable me to check him out and after an hour or so I had made my mind up to give him the 10 kilos to clear as long as he checked out with the people we had talked of. I didn't say anything then, and we arranged to meet the next day at his house so that I would know his whereabouts and we could talk more.

Within three hours of that meeting I had seen two of the guys we had talked of and they had put me at ease about Alan. So, within ten minutes of arriving at his house the next day, I had put forward my offer of giving him the 10 kilos on credit until December at £25,000 per kilo. Of course, he jumped at it. It was a good deal – he would make a minimum of £50,000 and possibly £100,000 if he worked it carefully. I left after arranging the details of the drop so that all I would have to do when I was ready was to ring him and say one word – 'Yes' – and it would be on. We also arranged the date and place where we would meet in December for him to hand over my £250,000.

The next week I went to meet Terry on the railway bridge feeling very relaxed, I had not tumbled any observations, although there was a problem: it was pouring with rain. You set up these meetings thinking it will appear normal to be standing on a bridge waiting to meet someone and having a chat, but to stand around in the pouring rain for any period of time definitely looks suspicious. So besides getting very wet, I was getting very twitchy when Terry turned up fifteen minutes late.

We went to a pub nearby. Terry seemed very relaxed, assuring me that everything had been alright and that he had had no intimations of being followed. I told him about what had happened in Berlin, but he wasn't bothered after I revealed that no one had been busted and that nothing had been found. I told him that I wanted to get my 10 kilos from him the next day and he said fine, so we set up a meet.

Then he gave me the bad news. He had not been able to arrange the burgling of the agency to remove the agreement I had signed. I was pissed off at the news, though I didn't let it show, because I could tell from the way he told me that he just couldn't bothered to do anything about it and had obviously thought I was being over-paranoid. The trouble was, I was beginning to feel that maybe I was being too paranoid. After all, I hadn't had any evidence of being watched for two months and although I knew of the bust in Germany, nothing had happened. Maybe I should relax. 'Fuck it, let it go,' I thought to myself, and left it at that.

The next morning's meet went like clockwork. I went for a long walk, making sure I wasn't followed, and met Terry at 10 o'clock as prearranged in the café in Battersea, where he gave me the keys to a hire car. I took the hire car and drove a few streets to another café, where Alan was sitting in the window, drinking a coffee and waiting for me. He came out and jumped in and we went for a spin round the block, just to make sure no one was watching. When he got out he went to the boot, took out a hold-all containing the 10 kilos and walked off to where his car was parked. I shot off and was back in the café where Terry was before my bacon sarnie had gone cold. All very neat and tidy.

Terry and I had a chat and agreed that we wouldn't contact one another until the beginning of April. We talked of hopefully getting things up and running again, but neither of us wanted to rush for the moment and with a cursory wave to each other he drove off in the hire car and I turned and walked home feeling very pleased that everything had been sorted neatly and efficiently. All that remained now was the little matter of collecting my £0.25 million on December 8. No problem.

My only other hassle was the company. Eddie was extremely pissed – not only had I been away for a month, but for the two weeks I'd been back I had been on the missing list more times than not. So I went home, picked up my car and went off to the yard in Kings Cross and settled into a routine of early nights and long days of work.

The next two months flew by. We were really busy at work and Mary and I seemed to be going out to parties and do's a hell of a lot. The problems hadn't affected our social life, as all of our friends were people with straight jobs or businesses. I must admit, I did still have a few ounces of my own coke stashed with a friend, so we were still partying but I was careful (well, sort of). The whole of the Peruvian problem was slowly receding, or at least I wasn't conscious of it all the time, and although I was still ultra-aware about checking for anyone following me, the paranoia was settling back to an amber level rather than a code red full alert.

Then, the last Saturday in November, Mary and I were having dinner in a wonderful restaurant called L'Arlequin on Queenstown Road when I suddenly had the most horrendous pains in my chest and had to go home. Within two hours I was in hospital with pneumonia.

I had obviously been seriously stressed out and what with working so hard, something had to give – and it was my body. The next week was spent on a drip , with a lot of discomfort but nothing serious other than a feeling of being totally exhausted. I got up and walked around the ward only to be shattered by the time I got back to my bed.

Mary was in looking after me all the time, along with a constant stream of visitors. Of course, after five days I was beginning to get worried, as I had my meeting to collect my money on the eighth of the month and as you can imagine I didn't want to miss that. So the day prior to the meeting I told Mary that I was going to discharge myself and rest up at home. After a bit of a row, she drove me from St Stephens in the Fulham Road back to our place. I collapsed into bed knackered from the climb up the stairs to our apartment on the first floor. Madam wasn't too impressed with that, and tried to talk me into going back to the hospital, but I convinced her I would get better more quickly now I was home and in our own bed. I slept the sleep of the just that night and woke up feeling fine, though tired.

Mary told me she would take the day off work if I wanted, but I definitely didn't want that, as my meeting with Alan and the money was arranged for one o'clock in Knightsbridge. I said I'd be fine, and off she went at about eight o'clock.

I got up about eleven, had a bath and got dressed and I was fucked when I was done. Still, I had to go for this meeting, and at about 12.15 made my way down to my car like some rusty old man and headed for Knightsbridge. My plan was that once I had the money I would go to a safety deposit box I had over in the City, stash the money, go home and collapse. Then, just as I pulled up next to Alan's Merc round the back of Knightsbridge, I remembered I had left the bloody key with my brother in Fulham. Alan got into the car with a large briefcase in his hands, looked at me and said:

'You look fucking awful!'

I felt it at that moment. I was feeling like shit and I'd forgotten the key. I couldn't even enjoy the fact that Alan was there and, from his demeanour, obviously had the dosh. I remember sitting there just wanting to be back in my bed, as Alan was raving on somewhere a million miles away through a cloud of tiredness about how well it had all gone and when could we do it again.

I turned to him. 'Alan, I feel really ill,' I began. 'I only came out of hospital yesterday – I've had pneumonia. Could you hang on to the money and I'll meet you here next week? I've got to get back to bed.'

'Don't worry. It'll be cool,' he assured me. 'Sure I'll see you here next week. Are you sure you don't want me to drive you home?'

'No I'll be alright.'

He clambered out of the car, looked back in with concern in his face and said: 'You look after yourself and I'll see you next week. Same time. Same place.' With that he waved, smiled and turned back towards his car.

I drove home and got back into bed, knackered. I had obviously pushed it too much. However, I was on the mend and within two days I was feeling fine again.

Mary and I were sitting in bed at about ten o'clock that night when the phone went. I leant over and picked it up.

'Is that Bob?' asked a voice I didn't recognise.

'Yes,' I answered. The line went dead.

I turned to Mary and said, 'That was weird.'

As the words left my lips that there was a knock on our

flat door. I thought it must be the porter and went to the door and looked through the spyhole. I knew immediately who the two guys were. I didn't recognise them personally, but it was them. 'We're being raided, stay cool,' I told Mary as they started to bang on the door. I opened it.

'Bob we've a search warrant can we come in?' said Laughing Boy Number One.

* * *

They were Customs and Excise, there were ten of them and they were very polite.

They allowed us to dress without searching our clothes first, which was lucky as I had my £2,000 float in the back pocket of my jeans. We were then taken into the living room while they rifled through drawers and cupboards. They found nothing and they didn't lift any floorboards, which again was lucky, as I had brought £10,000 from a friend's a few days before, thinking things were cooling down. I'd put it under the spare bedroom floor with the intention of taking it to the bank deposit with the money Alan had the following week.

We were then taken into the bedroom that had been searched while they searched the living room and I was able to slip the £2,000 from my pocket under a pillow on the bed.

They searched with no luck and acted as if they didn't expect any. After half an hour the boss came in and announced: 'I am charging you with conspiracy to import cocaine with persons and persons unknown.' That was it.

I was nicked, taken to the customs office in Fetter Lane and questioned for two days.

There was no tough questioning. It was obvious they had made a case before arresting me and during those two days I was able to fit into place all those missing pieces of the jigsaw that had been bothering me for the last six months.

The customs story had not started in London or Berlin with major surveillance and guns, but with the manager of a small bank in Shanklin on the Isle of Wight, of all places. One day he was looking at his customer's deposits and spotted an anomaly. Martha's English husband came from Shanklin and still had an account in this bank. One day back in May, before I had met him, he or Martha had deposited £15,000 in cash into the account via a bank in London. They had done the thing I had told her and Coci they mustn't do under any circumstances – pay large amounts of cash into a British account. The manager, who had never had those amounts deposited into the account before and knew of the new laws regarding deposits of this size, contacted the authorities. And it all started from there.

The customs had picked up on Martha or her husband from that deposit and had been on her from June onwards. The German police picked her up every time she returned to Berlin and monitored her and the Berlin people. She was tracked back to Peru via Miami and watched there.

The second major missing piece of the jigsaw was that when the German police had busted the Berlin flat in August they had found one of the wheels. I know this sounds incredible, but the guy had actually kept one of those large cast wheels in his loft. To this day I cannot believe that anyone could have been that stupid, let alone strong enough, to have got something so heavy into his loft. Not only was he that stupid but he also kept all the documentation regarding the shipments to London – and that's truly mind-bogglingly stupid. That the Peruvians had chosen to not tell me this was beyond stupid – it was a betrayal.

Therefore, the English customs had been able to visit the office agency and retrieved the form I had filled in. (The form I had asked Terry to retrieve, remember?) They therefore had a line from Peru to me. And that was it.

Just to finish it off for them, when they busted the gay guy and his boyfriend the same evening as myself, they found a piece of paper with my phone number on it in a fruitbowl. When pressurised by customs, they had both agreed to tell everything they knew in court.

That was all of the pieces of the jigsaw that had been brought onto me by others. The one piece I had missed, and shouldn't have, was that they had followed me for a month before I had spotted them. Luckily for my distributors, they had never seen them. But they had seen me meeting with Terry regularly and he was busted as well. So after the two days, he and I were charged before magistrates.

Two years later I was serving sixteen years and Terry was serving twelve.

Boom! Boom!

AFTERWORD

EDDIE COWELL NEVER gave my wife a penny after I was arrested.

David Philpot broke his back the day before I was arrested and spent the rest of his life in a wheelchair. He died in March 2001 and is sadly missed.

Alan Stanton and Mona disappeared with my £250,000. He died in prison seven years later. To this day Mona denies having had any of the money.

Percy Raines has never made any effort to repay the money I lent him to buy the house on Siros or made any effort to share the house with us.

We lost our apartment in Prince of Wales Drive due to seizure laws.

The Peruvians, except for Coci, served sentences from one to five years.

The gay Peruvian and his boyfriend died of AIDS.

I have not seen Terry to speak to since Wandsworth prison in 1993. I did see him driving a car in Fulham in 2000, though.

I don't know what happened to Coci. Good luck to him.

Roly still runs the family estate.

Chris is a successful businessman.

Jackie died of heroin in 1989.

I was released on parole in June 1996 with a degree in psychology, a mind intact and no bitterness. I broke laws and knew it and as Mick said many years before, getting nicked is paying taxes. As always with taxes, though, it was far too much to pay.

You spend days, weeks and months doing nothing and then there is a sudden explosion of activity. Once you are in the thick of it the power of the adrenaline takes over. You spend your time looking and watching everybody and everything.

Then you are driving across town with a carload and everything is OK. The money comes rolling in by the carrier bag full and you are out every night getting smashed and enjoying yourself. You go on holiday for a month and lap up the sunshine and think this is the life. You start a business that you think is going to be your passport to a normal life or the means of giving you enough cover to feel that you are safe. Then you find that your straight business partners regard you as a cash cow and you are lazy and let it go. You then find you are down to your last ten grand. So you phone a friend and you are off again wheeling and dealing. Then you get busted.

Well, that is how it seems to have gone for me. I don't think I'm a fool but as I sit here and try to rationalise my thirty years of involvement, I am not quite so sure. I never consciously considered whether it was a wise choice to be a drugs scammer; I was just in there doing it. When I was in prison I was so busy trying to survive the ennui and mindlessness of it that it was impossible to feel that you were in any way at fault in your choice of life when you were being subjugated to a spiteful vindictiveness – which, unless you have experienced it, you cannot believe possible. When you were doing it there was no time for introspection, or should I say, no wish for it.

I leave you to judge the wisdom or not of my choice of life.